Understanding primary science

05

2005

QUESTIONS
PUBLISHING
COMPANY

Understanding primary science

Subject knowledge and sample lesson plans for Key Stages 1 and 2

Roy Phipps

The Questions Publishing Company Ltd
Birmingham
2002

First published in 2000 by
The Questions Publishing Company Ltd
Leonard House, 321 Bradford Street,
Digbeth, Birmingham B5 6ET

© 2002 Roy Phipps

Edited by Diane Parkin
Designed by Al Stewart
Typeset in Garamond
Cover design by Lisa Martin
Illustrations by Pat Murray, Graham Cameron Illustration

About the author

Roy Phipps is a senior lecturer in Science Education, Bretton Hall, College of the University of Leeds, Wakefield where he works on primary initial teacher training courses. He also co-ordinates the Bretton Hall AstraZeneca Science Teaching Project working within Barnsley LEA. This is a Millennium project funded by the AstraZeneca Science Teaching Trust. He has written several articles and is also a co-author with Rosemary Feasey, Anne Goldsworthy and John Stringer of *Star Science*, a primary science scheme from Ginn & Co.

Acknowledgements

I wish to thank Glyn Denton, a student at Bretton Hall for his comments on the draft manuscripts for the introduction; my wife Anne for the time sacrifices she has made while I wrote this and other works, and for her support in reading, commenting on and correcting the original drafts. This book is dedicated to her as well as Alison, Robert, Andrew and Nicola, who may be more influential than me in the 21st century.

Contents

Introduction: personal knowledge and ideas for teaching scientific enquiry

Introduction

How to use this book: personal knowledge and ideas for teaching Scientific Enquiry (Sc1)

The DfEE responded in 1998, after years of pleas from primary teachers for support with curriculum planning in primary science, by jointly working with the Qualifications and Curriculum Authority (QCA) to write guidance in the form of a scheme of work for science for Key Stages 1 and 2. This is non-statutory but intended to be supportive. It offers guidance on how:

▲ the statutory content of science in the National Curriculum can be delivered by suggesting a curriculum map to ensure coverage of the programmes of study for Years 1 to 6;

▲ the programmes of study for Sc1, Scientific Enquiry, can be integrated in the programmes of study which focus on knowledge, i.e. Sc2 Life Processes and Living Things, Sc3 Materials and their Properties and Sc4 Physical Processes;

▲ to sequence the teaching – a suggested list of a sequence of activities helps to develop children's conceptual and procedural understanding in science;

▲ science can contribute to the development of other aspects of the primary curriculum especially in literacy and numeracy and information and communication technology (ICT).

Need for lesson plans

QCA's scheme of work **does not** provide detailed lesson plans. This book is intended to offer the teacher and student teacher further insights into interpreting the **possible** activities suggested in the detailed scheme of work with a series of sample **lesson plans**. For each theme a lesson plan is provided for Reception, Year1/2, Year 3/4 and Year 5/6. The lesson plans give the student in Initial Teacher Training support by offering a format which will help them meet the requirements of the Initial Teacher Training for Primary Science on planning individual science lessons and sequences of lessons. (Annex E of DfEE Circular 4/98 p 12). The format suggested can be fine-tuned to meet format requirements of different teacher training institutions for students' lesson plans. The plans will also support teachers in primary schools who feel less confident with aspects of subject knowledge.

In some cases I have suggested quite **different** activities to those in the QCA scheme of work yet they still meet the same learning objectives. QCA suggests that teachers amend or add their own material to the scheme of work. Tried and tested lesson plans should not be abandoned because they are not explicitly in the QCA scheme of work.

Each lesson plan contains the following:

- ▲ the learning objectives for the children;
- ▲ how the teacher might introduce the lesson;
- ▲ what the children should do during the lesson;
- ▲ a plenary session – how the children's learning can be reviewed at the end of the lesson.

There are also suggestions in the form of questions which teachers can use to assess the learning that has taken place during the lesson.

Teachers' personal knowledge and understanding of science

Many primary teachers need support with their personal subject knowledge. To teach confidently, teachers need to feel secure with their own factual subject knowledge for each theme to be taught. This may require pre-lesson research in the form of reading to either learn or refresh the accuracy of subject knowledge. I still do this for my lessons after many years of teaching science, even though I have a science degree. To support you, either as a student or teacher, each theme in the book has background subject knowledge for that theme which will develop your knowledge and understanding beyond that needed by pupils.

Teachers need both factual knowledge and a secure understanding of the procedures of Sc1, Scientific Enquiry, in the National Curriculum. You need to be familiar with strategies for planning, obtaining evidence from carrying out enquiries and investigations, and very importantly, how to make use of the evidence collected. Different strategies should be used for different stages and all teachers need to be familiar with these. Knowing about and understanding the lines of progression for different aspects of Sc1 will support you in planning and in providing differentiated practical activities. It will make this aspect of the curriculum accessible and enjoyable for both you and the children.

The introductory section in the book supports the development of a personal understanding of Sc1. Key points have been carefully embedded in the subsequent lesson plans to illustrate how Sc1 can be progressed through the primary years. Sc1 cannot be taught without a **context**. Themes such as plants, sound, forces, etc. provide contexts. When planning lessons for any context you should:

- ▲ check the content to be covered from the programme of study;
- ▲ think about **how** aspects of Sc1, Scientific Enquiry, can contribute to the sequence of lessons when planning a scheme of work and especially when planning learning objectives.

Remember that currently at KS1, Sc1

still has an assessment weighting of 50% and at KS2, a 40% weighting. It is very important and needs to be systematically planned and taught.

The Government has recently established a statutory curriculum for initial teacher training in science and this became a legal requirement in September 1999. Annex E of DfEE Circular 4/98 identifies the knowledge and skills that trainee teachers need to gain to satisfy the science standards for gaining qualified teacher status. This book, with the sample model lessons, is intended to help trainee teachers on their journey towards achieving qualified teacher status.

Personal knowledge and ideas for teaching Sc1 Scientific Enquiry

Sc1 gives children the opportunity to experience the **processes** and **skills** of science. It includes the development of the following process skills:

▲ observing;
▲ raising questions;
▲ predicting and hypothesising;
▲ planning and carrying out investigations;
▲ measuring;
▲ recording;
▲ considering evidence;
▲ communicating.

Observation involves using all the senses. For young children it is very important that they have time to observe and that they are encouraged to use all their senses when it is safe to do so. It may not always be safe to explore using taste or smell, e.g. when exploring soil. Given time to explore and play, children should be encouraged to **raise questions**. These should be shared and used by the teacher to select those questions that can be investigated. Your skill in questioning is important. You need to be able to **modify children's ideas and questions into a form that can be investigated**. Children should be encouraged to make **predictions** about what they think will happen in an investigation. By asking them to explain their prediction they will be encouraged to convert it into a **hypothesis**, usually by using the connective 'because'.

The following illustrates the difference between these terms.

Teacher: 'What do you think will happen if I drop these two balls?'
Child: 'The red ball will bounce higher.'
This is a prediction.
Teacher: 'Why?'
Child: 'Because the red ball is made of rubber and it bounces better than sponge, which is what the yellow ball is made of.' *This is a hypothesis.*

Predictions can be incorporated into **planning investigations**.

Planning investigations effectively requires the teacher to have knowledge and understanding of what an investigation is. Investigations are different from other forms of practical work. The special features of investigations include children either working closely with a teacher or independently:

▲ making their own decisions;
▲ planning either with teacher support or independently;

▲ identifying which factors to change, which to measure and which to keep the same to make a test fair;
▲ choosing equipment and using it appropriately;
▲ applying existing science knowledge to develop their scientific understanding.

Investigations need a context and are best introduced when children have been taught and have developed some science knowledge concepts first. This knowledge is then used in an investigation. The investigation enables concepts and process skills to be used together to find out something which the children do not know the answer to. There may be more than one way of finding out the answer.

Subject knowledge needed to teach Sc1 confidently

Science in the National Curriculum for Key Stages 1 and 2 refers to fair tests and states that 'changing one factor and observing or measuring the effect, while keeping other factors the same, allows a fair test or comparison to be made'. However, the Initial Teacher Training National Curriculum (ITTNC) (1998) requires trainee teachers to know and understand the 'factors' in an investigation in terms of 'the nature of variables including the identification of **categoric**, **independent** and **dependent variables**, recognition of **discrete** and **continuous variables**' (TTA 1998 p17).

A working knowledge of variables is the key to understanding the nature of scientific investigations and enquiry. If you are unsure whether an activity is an investigation or not, you need to check it for **three salient features**. If it is an investigation it will have:

▲ the factor you are systematically changing and investigating – this is the **independent variable**;
▲ the factor you observe, measure or judge to answer the question you are investigating – this is the **dependent variable**;
▲ the factor(s) to keep the same to make the test fair – **the control variable(s)**.

Now try this (but first cover up the table opposite)

In the following example undertaken by a student teacher with Key Stage 1 children, the investigation is analysed to illustrate the variables in an investigation. The student teacher had raised a question for the children to investigate. She also offered lots of teacher support. Her question was:

'How does the number of presents change the pull force needed to move Santa's sledge?' (**Figure 1**)

First carry out **a variable scan** of this question:

What is the independent variable?
What is the dependent variable?
If these two kinds of variables are embedded in the question then you have a question that can be investigated.

Now decide what you would keep the same to make the test fair. What are these variables called?

Analysis of variables for the investigation

How does the number of presents change the pull force needed to pull Santa's sledge?

What we will systematically change (**independent variable**)	What we will judge or measure to answer the question being investigated (**dependent variable**)	What we will keep the same to make the test fair (**control variables**)
The number of presents on the sledge	The force needed to pull the sledge with different numbers of presents on it	▲ the sledge ▲ the surface for pulling the sledge ▲ the size of the presents (e.g. volume and mass)

Answer:
All questions to be investigated can be analysed in this way. The independent variable and dependent variable are the **key variables** – in this case the number of presents and the size of the pull force.

In primary science you will usually work with three kinds of variables. These are:

1. **Categoric.** This is when the variable is a 'clear-cut' category, e.g. boy or girl, colour, shape, type of material such as wool, cotton, nylon or in the Santa's sledge investigation, it would be the presents.
2. **Discrete.** These are variables that have only **whole number values** (1, 2, 3, etc.), e.g. the number of layers of insulation on a bottle of hot water; the number of holes in a parachute or, in the Santa's sledge investigation, the number of presents. All these discrete variables are represented by whole numbers.
3. **Continuous.** These are variables that can have any values and involve measuring with standard measures, e.g. in another sledge investigation the question being investigated might be: 'How does changing the mass on the sledge affect the pull force needed to move it?'

The mass can have any value, would be measured in grams and the pull force would be measured with a Newton meter in Newtons.

Figure 1

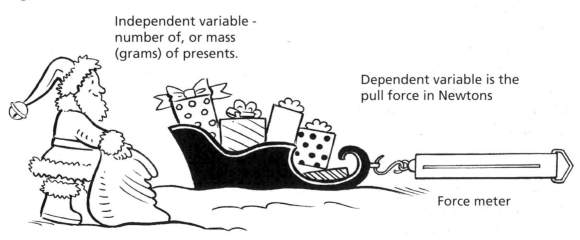

Independent variable - number of, or mass (grams) of presents.

Dependent variable is the pull force in Newtons

Force meter

Planning investigations at Key Stage 1

Children at both Key Stages require support in planning investigations. At Key Stage 1 planning frameworks have been developed to scaffold children's learning. In *Star Science* (Feasey, Goldsworthy, Phipps and Stringer 1997) from Ginn & Co, a planning house framework has been devised mainly to help teachers to plan investigations by focusing on the salient points of the investigation. It is presented in the shape of a house with different storeys. Each storey has a question to help the teacher elicit and record children's ideas about what to do at different stages in the investigation. Dri-wipe pens and acetate overlays on the actual framework allow the resources to be re-used (**Figure 2**).

The focus questions are:

What do we want to find out?
How will we do it?
What will we need?
How will we make it fair?
What have we found out?

Figure 2

The focus questions can be changed. For example, if the teacher is encouraging the skill of predicting then an extra question could be included such as: 'What do you think will happen?' And if fostering hypothesising: 'Why do you think that?'

This framework can be used at the planning stage and also at the plenary or reviewing stage.

For the Santa's sledge investigation a completed one may look like this:

What do we want to find out? How the extra presents change the pull force needed to move Santa's sledge.

How will we do it? Put presents one at a time on the sledge and use a 'pull meter' to see how the pull changes each time.

What will we need? Sledge, presents, force or pull meter.

How will we make it fair? Only try it on the table, keep presents the same shape and weight.

What have we found out? The more presents on the sledge the bigger the pull force needed to move the sledge.

For different **contexts** of investigation a different contextual format could be developed and used, e.g. if planning work on **change and baking**, a planning cake can be devised on the same lines. A large card circle can be divided into segments, labelled with salient questions, covered with transparent plastic and cut into segments. As each question is considered and scribed by the teacher, the cake is 'assembled' to give a record of the plan and the answer to the question being investigated (**Figure 3**).

Figure 3

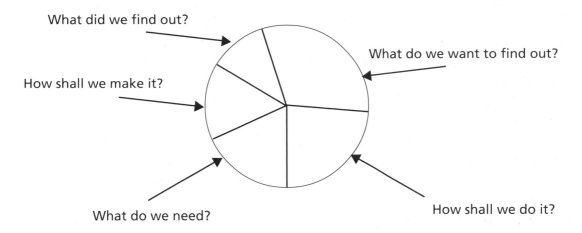

It could be mounted with Velcro or Blu-tack on either fabric or other surfaces for whole class teaching and displayed as evidence of children's ideas of planning.

Ideas for other contextual planning frameworks:

▲ planning flower (plants and plant growth);
▲ planning Christmas tree (for investigating conductors and insulators which make a bulb light; you could actually have a circuit connected to the plan so that the conductors light the bulb at the top of the planning tree).

Such approaches scaffold children's learning and support teachers in focusing on the key points in an investigation.

Planning investigations at Key Stage 2

Planning boards can be designed that focus on both planning and recording. If these are made A3 size, one side of the board can be for planning and the other for recording (**Figures** 4 and 5). A different coloured paper could be used for differentiating the focus. To make these boards use text and questions such as:

Figure 4
Planning board

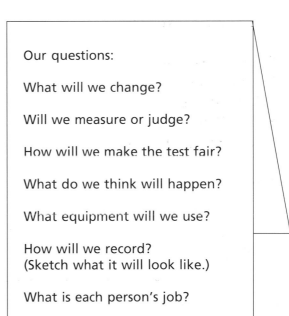

Planning and reporting boards can be prepared on A3 paper, mounted on card, laminated and then used many times with dri-wipe pens. They can be placed by the side of equipment used by children to display and therefore

Figure 5
Reporting board

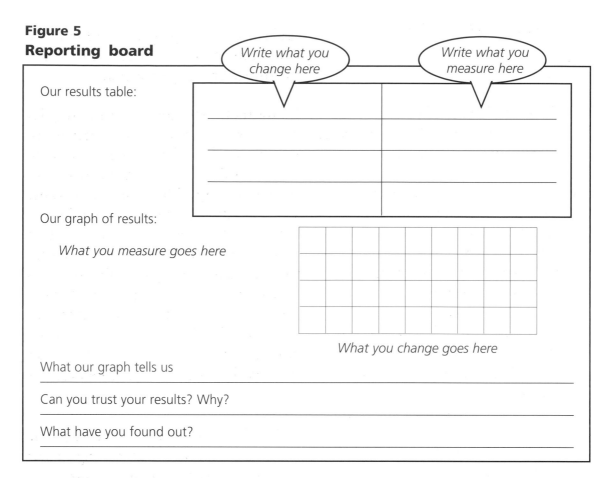

Our results table:

> *Write what you change here*

> *Write what you measure here*

Our graph of results:

What you measure goes here

What you change goes here

What our graph tells us

Can you trust your results? Why?

What have you found out?

demonstrate children's experience of scientific enquiry. This can be a support to the teacher in the early stages of teaching investigations and gives status to scientific enquiry in the classroom (**Figures 5** and **6**).

Figure 6

Using tables for planning and recording scientific enquiries

Tables encourage children to be systematic in their planning and recording. Children need to be taught

how to use them, and experience using them on a regular basis.

A two-column table (**Figure** 7) gives a structure to an investigation. Consider the Santa's sledge investigation. At the planning stage the children decided to systematically increase the number of presents on the sledge and to measure the pull force to move the sledge.

Figure 7

Number of presents	Pull force in Newtons
1	
2	
3	

Advantages of tables

Tables:

▲ show what to change – the independent variable – and what to measure – the dependent variable;

▲ show what sequence to follow;

▲ show how to start and end the investigation;

▲ show how to organise the evidence in an orderly manner so that observations can be easily compared;

▲ encourage use of measurements collected as evidence for answering the question being investigated;

▲ foster the use of evidence for seeing patterns and drawing conclusions which may raise further questions to be investigated;

▲ enable evidence collected to be used systematically for drawing graphs.

Science process skills fostered through using tables include:

▲ planning;

▲ observing and measuring;

▲ recording systematically;

▲ considering evidence;

▲ communicating findings.

At Key Stage 1 and in lower Key Stage 2 children will need teacher support in learning how to use tables and appreciate their use. Large, re-useable two column table formats can be made along similar lines to the suggestions for making planning boards. Outline tables, mounted on card and laminated, can be used over and over again with dri-wipe pens. Children can contribute to the recording process at the direction of the teacher.

Using tables should feature at regular intervals in the science curriculum, especially when the key objective is to teach children how to plan or record systematically. The completed table can be displayed to provide evidence that children have experienced this aspect of the curriculum. Older children should be given table outlines to save time in drawing them. It is the skill of using tables for planning and recording that is fostered, **not** drawing skills of making neat tables which take some children a considerable amount of time.

By Y6 children should be making their own tables that foster recording repeat readings of the dependent variable. The following example is a suitable format and maintains the correct location of the independent and dependent variable.

Key Stage 1 and lower Key Stage 2

A teacher-produced table at Key Stage 1 may involve children individually but, with teacher support, contribute by adding data to parts of it (**Figure 8**).

At lower Key Stage 2, children should use teacher-prepared outlines, e.g. photocopied blank table formats to add the independent and dependent variables, and their own observations and measurements (**Figure 9**).

Upper Key Stage 2

By encouraging this format for recording there is consistency in a

Figure 8
Key Stage 1 and lower Key Stage 2

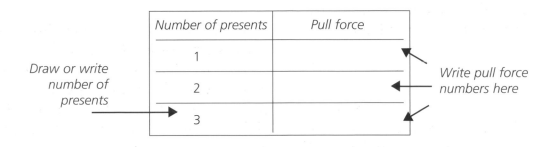

Number of presents	Pull force
1	
2	
3	

Draw or write number of presents

Write pull force numbers here

Figure 9
Lower Key Stage 2

Children add own headings to columns

Figure 10
Upper Key Stage 2

Independent variable could have any number value. Therefore continuous

Dependent variable. Can have any number value

Mass of presents (g)	Pull force needed to move sledge (N)			
	First reading	Second reading	Third reading	Average
100				
200				
300				
400				

school's approach to using tables for both planning and recording and children are less likely to become confused. They will learn the procedure by revisiting this process in a variety of contexts (**Figure 10**).

Developing graphing skills

Reception and KS1

Pictograms, in my experience, provide the best way to introduce children to developing graphing skills. Surveys are ideal contexts. The teacher and children can collect information together. For example, a survey could be done about favourite fruits.

Which fruits do our class like best?

Children can draw a picture of a fruit they like and colour it in on a square of paper approximately 5cm". The teacher co-ordinates the range of responses, listing each fruit on the board in a two-column table (see diagram). She now teaches the children how to use the fruit pictures to tell 'the story of their survey' by involving the children in making a pictogram.

Fruit	Number of children
Draw and write 'Strawberry'	ЖЖ I = 6
Draw and write 'Peach' etc	IIII = 4 etc

The teacher then explains another way of showing this information. S/he has prepared an outline of a graph with two axes and made 'faintly drawn squares' about the same size as the paper children have drawn their favourite fruit on.

S/he looks at all the fruits in the survey and adds a ready drawn picture of each on the x axis, leaving a gap between each category or type. Type of fruit is an example of a **categoric variable**. The fruits are unrelated so a gap is left between them, just as Mori opinion polls shown on the television news at election times about political

opinion show gaps between the main political parties (**Figure 11**).

The teacher chooses a child and discusses his or her favourite fruit and shows the class where it fits on the graph. Some glue is then applied to the picture and, with teacher support, the child adds his or her fruit to the graph. The teacher repeats this whole class demonstration with another child. Every child then has an opportunity to add his or her fruit picture to the graph.

Figure 11

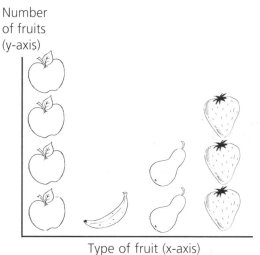

Number of fruits (y-axis)

Type of fruit (x-axis)

The teacher could explain that the class has made a pictogram that tells the story of their survey. S/he asks children simple questions about the pictogram. S/he starts with an easy question and makes them progressively harder, e.g:

1. How many favourite fruits are in our pictogram? (Answer is found by counting the number of categories on the x axis.)

2. Which is the favourite fruit in our class? (Answer will be the column with the most fruit pictures. Ask children to explain

their answer.)

3. Which is the least favourite fruit? (Answer will be the column with the least fruit pictures. Ask children to explain their answer.)

Such questions could be displayed by the pictogram and reconsidered again on future occasions. Children will need to repeat these skills if they are to learn to interpret graphs, just as they repeat reading skills and number skills. Graphing is important because it enables children to visually see **patterns and relationships** that lead to **generalisations about events**. Graphing skills should be consciously taught from an early stage using a framework such as that described here, and used in different contexts to reinforce children's learning.

The process should be repeated at suitable points until the teacher considers that ICT could be introduced as an alternative, e.g. *My World* and *Survey*. These are software packages that support children's early graphing skills. Children who physically engage in the process of contributing to making a graph will receive good foundations for developing this skill as they progress through school.

Block graphs are essentially the same as pictograms: square blocks but with no pictures. Again children can construct blocks manually with squares of coloured paper or with the aid of ICT, e.g. *My World* has a facility for block graphs (**Figure 12**).

Bar charts

At lower Key Stage 2, bar charts build on pictograms and block graphs.

A bar chart should help children see the effect of the independent variable (what they changed and investigated) on the dependent variable (what they measured to answer the question being investigated). At this stage children should be familiar with graph outlines and be taught to produce their

Figure 12
Example of a pictogram

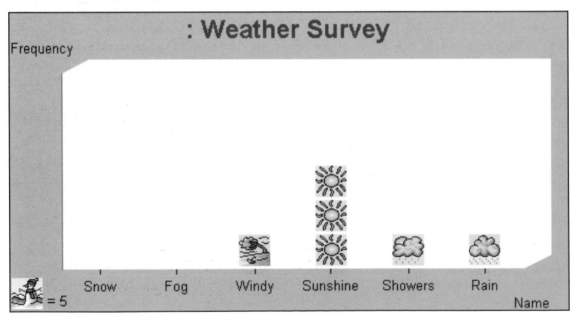

own. If data has been recorded in a table, with correct headings, then they can be taught how to use the data to make a graph (**Figure 13**).

Example of using bar graphs

If we return to the Santa's sledge context and modify the question being investigated to: 'How does the surface affect the pull force needed to move a sledge?', the variables have been mentally manipulated to offer a different investigation. Children could change the surface to compare, e.g. wood, plastic and carpet – the type of surface is the independent variable and is categoric. They would use a force meter to measure the pull force – the dependent variable – and this will have a numerical value. The sledge and its load remain the same so they

are the control variables. A bar graph of the findings might look like **Figure 14**, overleaf.

There are gaps again between the bars because **type of surface** is a categoric variable. It never has a numerical value; only words are used. It is **qualitative** or **descriptive** information. Because of this only a bar graph is suitable. The scale has been added considering the **range of the values** of the force measurements collected during the investigation. The x and y axes have been labelled. The data have been ordered – biggest to smallest force value. A bar graph helps children to see an **order** of results as they consider the evidence.

Graphs should be analysed by a **progression of questions** that become harder.

Figure 13
Connection between tables and graphs

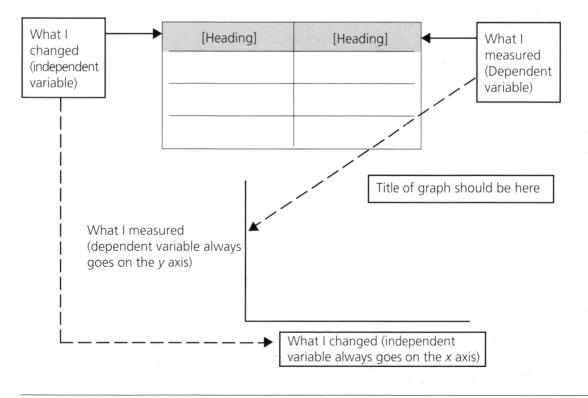

Figure 14
How the surface affects the pull force needed to move the sledge

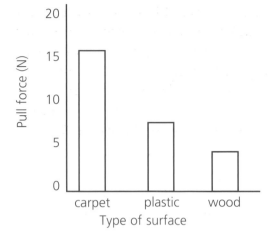

For example:

1. How many surfaces were tested?
   (Requires child to read the number of data points.)
2. Which was the hardest surface to pull the sledge over?
   (Requires child to read the maximum value.)
3. Which was the easiest surface to pull the sledge over?
   (Requires child to read the minimum value.)
4. How much force did it take to move the sledge on the carpet?
   (Requires child to read the data point on a grid line.)
5. How much harder was it to move the sledge on the carpet than the wood?
   (Requires child to read the difference between two fixed points.)

A framework of questions like this should be used in many contexts to help children develop the skill of **considering and evaluating evidence**. It can be practised as a paper and pencil activity, but will be most meaningful when children consider evidence in graphs constructed from data they have collected during their own scientific enquiries.

Line graphs

By upper Key Stage 2 children should be collecting information to draw line graphs from their investigation. It is a requirement in Sc1 at level 5. So what are the rules or principles for drawing line graphs?

Line graphs can only be produced from two sets of data that are **continuous**, i.e. which can have **any numerical value**. This means that **measurements** have to be made for both the independent and the dependent variables.

If we return to our sledge enquiries that have progressed from KS1, then the same equipment could be used for an investigation, but with greater demand simply by changing the question so that it requires two sets of continuous data to be collected. This is an investigation at a higher level. A possible question might be: 'How does the mass (weight) on the sledge affect the pull force needed to move it?'

In this investigation children could use objects and find their mass using a balance. They would add objects – more than four – of known masses systematically to the sledge and measure the force needed to move it over one type of surface (control variable) such as the pupils' work-table or desk. Mass and force can be of any value and only a line graph should be drawn (**Figure 15**). It is the mass on the sledge that is systematically changed – the independent variable –

and the force to move it is the dependent variable. These are the **key factors** that form the investigation.

Figure 15

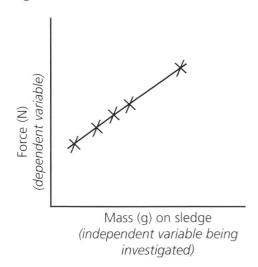

Force (N)
(dependent variable)

Mass (g) on sledge
(independent variable being investigated)

Line graphs are harder for children because they have to 'manage' the handling of at least two sets of numbers. They are produced from numerical **quantitative** data only. This is why they are more difficult than bar graphs where children only have to handle one set of numerical data for the dependent variable.

Line graphs also tell the story of an event. They show relationships between factors that are changed and being investigated. Children should learn to interrogate them through questioning which will encourage them to make predictions. They can

extrapolate, i.e. extend the line to make predictions about values which were outside the range of their original measurements. They can **interpolate** and make predictions about values that lie between two points on the actual line graph, i.e. between points that were within their measurement range even though not actually measured in their investigations (**Figure 16**).

Summary

Key questions for the teacher:

When do I use a bar graph? When do I use a line graph?

A **bar graph** is drawn when the independent variable – the factor you change and which you are investigating – is a category. Categories can only be described in words, i.e. **qualitatively**. A bar graph always has a gap between each category.

A **line graph** is drawn when both the factor being changed and investigated (the independent variable) and the factor being measured (the dependent variable) are both continuous and have any numerical value.

Examples of continuous variables include mass, force, volume, temperature and time.

Progression in graph skills in scientific investigations and enquiries

Figure 16

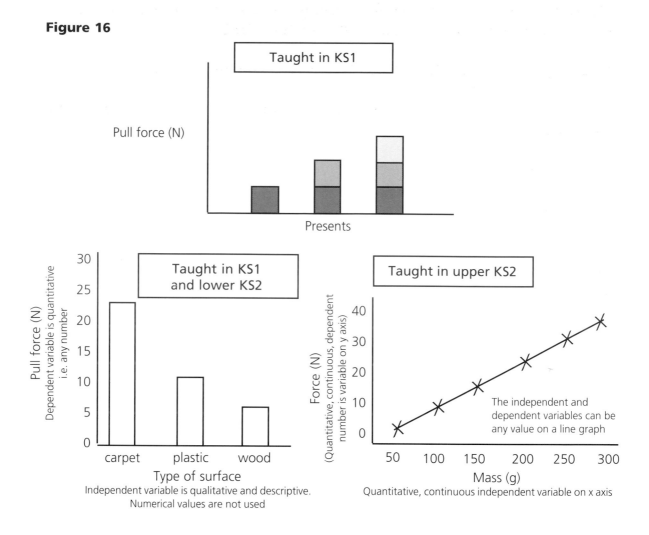

For level 5 to be achieved, pupils need to plot **more than 3** points on their line graph.

Watch out for ICT graphing programmes.

Some ICT software programmes currently on the market enable data collection to be presented as graphs. ICT programmes may offer children a range of the same options for graph types: bar graphs, line graphs, and pie charts, regardless of the types of data children have collected. Pie charts are not necessary or relevant for considering scientific evidence at KS1 or 2, and they are not mentioned in the science National Curriculum. Switching between bar graphs and line graphs indiscriminately is not going to reinforce accepted procedures. The teacher and student trainee must have subject knowledge of which graph to choose, based on a personal knowledge and understanding of the graphing demands of their scientific investigations and enquiries. S/he should use this knowledge to ensure enquiries are differentiated to meet the needs of children's different stages and abilities.

Bibliography

DfEE/TTA (1998) *Initial teacher training National Curriculum for primary science* (Annex E of DfEE Circular 4/98) London: DfEE.

DFE (1995) *Science in the National Curriculum* London: HMSO.

Feasey, R., Goldsworthy, A., Phipps, R. and Stringer, J. (1997) *Star Science* Aylesbury: Ginn & Co.

ICT Resources:

Survey from:
SPA
PO Box 59
Tewkesbury
Gloucestershire
GL20 6AB

Chapter 1
Plants

There are different kinds of plants. Much of the work in the National Curriculum on plants can be done with plants that flower and produce seeds to maintain their life cycle. Some plants do not flower but should be encountered during the study of the environment and the variety of life. They include:

▲ algae, which include sea weeds;
▲ mosses and liverworts, which have small leaves and stems but reproduce by making spores;
▲ ferns, which have fronds that look like leaves – the lower-side of a fern frond produces spores for reproduction;
▲ conifer trees, e.g. Christmas trees, which make cones that contain seeds for continuing the life cycle.

Plant cells

All plants are made of **cells**. A cell is the basic structure of a living thing. Some algae are composed of a single plant cell, but most are many-celled or **multi-cellular**. Plant cells, e.g. onion skin, need to be viewed under a microscope (see **Figure 17**) to see their structural components, and under an electron microscope to see very

great detail of the cell's structure. The parts of a plant perform different functions.

Figure 17

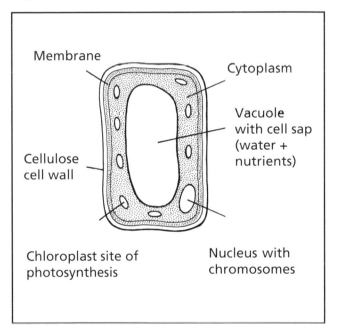

Membrane
Cytoplasm
Vacuole with cell sap (water + nutrients)
Cellulose cell wall
Chloroplast site of photosynthesis
Nucleus with chromosomes

The dead **cellulose wall** gives the plant cell a fairly rigid structure. This wall is lined on the inside by the **cytoplasm** that is living, jelly-like material. This is where the life processes of respiration, growth, etc, occur. In some cells exposed to light, there are small green structures called **chloroplasts** in the cytoplasm. Chloroplasts can trap light energy and convert it into food energy in a process called **photosynthesis**. In green plants it is the blue and red parts of the visible spectrum that are absorbed and green light is reflected. This is why most plants look green.

The **vacuole** is a container of **sap**. Sap is mostly water with some dissolved nutrients such as sugars, nitrates, magnesium, etc. This watery fluid pushes the membrane against the cell wall and keeps the plant cell turgid. The membrane allows some substances to enter and leave the cell. In a whole plant consisting of many cells, the turgid force is important in supporting it and keeping it upright. During drought or loss of water there is less fluid in the vacuoles and the plant wilts and becomes unable to support itself. The **nucleus** controls the activities of the cell. It contains **chromosomes** that are thread-like bodies made of deoxyribonucleic acid or **DNA** for short.

DNA is the genetic material that all living things inherit from their parents and it determines their characteristics. It contains all the information needed for a cell and therefore the whole living thing to live. The information can be thought of as a chemical code. **Genes** code the cell to make chemicals such as different proteins. The end product of all the genetic codes determines a living thing's characteristics, e.g. height of plant, colour of flower, shape of flower, type of root, etc. Parts of chromosomes are passed on from one generation to the next during sexual reproduction.

Asexual reproduction and cloning

When a plant grows from a cutting (or an animal such as Dolly the sheep, where the nucleus of a parental body cell is placed into an egg cell that has had its nucleus removed), it does not involve the bringing together of different genes. (**Figure 18**) The new plant or animal is genetically identical to the parent plant. It has exactly the same genes as its parent and is an example of a **clone**. Clones are examples of asexual reproduction.

Figure 18

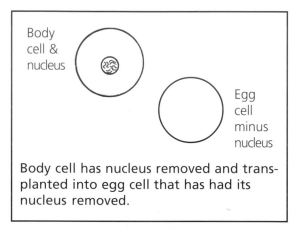

Body cell & nucleus

Egg cell minus nucleus

Body cell has nucleus removed and transplanted into egg cell that has had its nucleus removed.

The smallest section of a chromosome that can code for one characteristic is a gene. There are millions of different genes. Genes are being 'engineered' into living things to introduce new characteristics for human benefit. This is controversial; some people argue that it is for human benefit, while others disagree.

Germination

Flowering plants grow from **seeds**. The start of seed growth is called **germination**. A seed contains a food reserve and an **embryo** (baby) plant. Every seed is surrounded by a hard protective seed coat that helps it survive adverse conditions. In the coat there is a small opening to enable water and air to enter (**Figure 19**). To begin germinating a seed needs water. Germination is speeded up if it is warm. The process also needs air (oxygen) and the seed must be at a stage of maturity to begin growing. The embryo begins to digest the food (starch, protein and fats) stored in the seed when activated by water that enters the seed. Digested foods become simpler, e.g. starch is made into sugar, proteins into amino acids, and move from the food store into the embryo.

The embryo uses sugar for:

▲ respiration to give it energy to carry out life processes;
▲ making new plant cell walls.

Amino acids are used to make new cells (cytoplasm and nuclei) so the seed grows. While the seed is germinating it actually becomes lighter in mass as it respires the food reserves. It does not actually begin to make food until the embryonic leaves receive light. At this stage when photo-synthesis is greater than respiration, the mass of the plant increases and it grows by adding 'permanent bulk' rather than just temporary transient materials such as water.

There are two types of germination. Some plants have seed coats and embryonic leaves – **cotyledons** – that remain below the ground during germination. They include peas and beans and are examples of **hypogeal** germination. Others lift the seed coat above the ground during the germination process, e.g. onions and leeks. Sunflowers leave the seed coat just below the soil surface, but the cotyledons are lifted above the soil. The seed coat can often be seen on the first leaves of newly emergent plants and is an example of **epigeal** germination. (Remember 'e' for exit – seed coats exit from the soil.) If both types of seeds are used during teaching, children can be offered the opportunity to note similarities and differences based on focused observations.

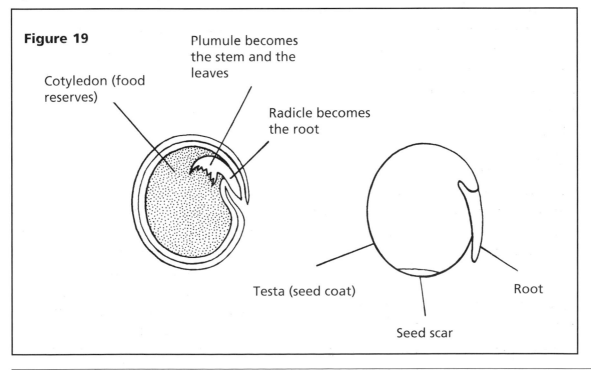

Figure 19

Cotyledon (food reserves)

Plumule becomes the stem and the leaves

Radicle becomes the root

Testa (seed coat)

Seed scar

Root

Parts and functions of flowering plants

Part	Function
Roots	▲ Anchor plant in soil ▲ Store surplus food, e.g. carrots and turnips are roots with stores of food ▲ Absorb water and nutrients from soil
Stem	▲ Supports the plant above the ground ▲ Carries water and nutrients to the leaves and flowers in special 'woody' tubes ▲ Carries food from leaves to the roots in phloem ▲ Supports the leaves and flowers
Leaves	▲ Take in carbon dioxide and give off oxygen in light conditions, through holes called stomata ▲ Use carbon dioxide, sunlight and water to make food by photosynthesis ▲ Allow water loss by transpiration to keep leaves cool
Flower	Often (but not always) has male and female parts within a single flower. ▲ Many have petals that are coloured and sweet smelling ▲ Male part – anther – makes pollen cells ▲ Female part – ovary – makes egg cells ▲ When pollen and egg join or fuse then a new embryo begins and a fruit develops that contains or bears seeds

Figure 20

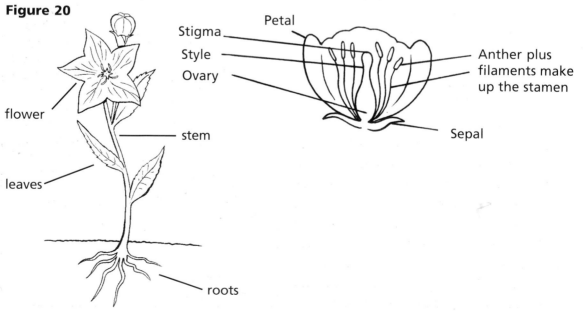

Pollination, fertilisation, seeds and fruits

There are two important processes in flowering plant reproduction.

Pollination is the transfer of pollen – the male sex cell – to the **stigma** of the female **carpel**. This is the first stage of bringing the male and female sex cells together. The stigma makes a sugary substance to help the pollen grain stick and to nourish it. The pollen grain germinates and makes a tube that grows into the neck of the carpel and down to the entrance of the **ovary** where the female sex cell – the **ovule** – is. The ovule and pollen cells each have half the number of chromosomes of other cells in the plant. The male cell fuses with the ovule to restore the requisite number of chromosomes for that species of plant. This is **fertilisation** (**Figure 21**).

anism for promoting variation within a species and this confers greater ability to survive changes in the environment. There is a greater likelihood of some members of the species surviving and therefore maintaining the species that can adapt to new conditions. This is a process of **natural selection**, the basis of Charles Darwin's theory of **evolution**.

Fruits and seeds

When pollen and egg cells join together the ovule has been **fertilised** and changes occur which lead to the development of a **seed** or seeds, usually within the ovary. The ovary develops into a **fruit**. For example, in a pea flower the ovary wall changes to become a pod which is the fruit, and inside it the peas that develop are the seeds that can give rise to the next generation (**Figure 22**).

Figure 21

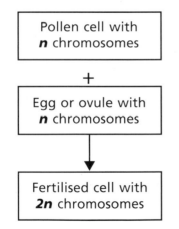

This new combination of chromosomes is copied or replicated as the fertilised cell develops into an **embryo** and eventually a plant. Thus all the plant cells receive copies of the same chromosomes. Only when sex cells are made is the number of chromosomes halved and the genes shuffled, so no two sex cells carry the same genes. Thus, sexual reproduction is a mech-

Figure 22

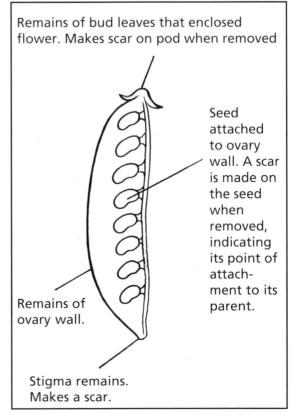

All fruits have two scars. You should be able to see these easily on oranges and grapefruit. The pin prick at one end is the remains of the stigma and if the button-like remains of the flower bud leaves are removed, another scar is evident. Fruits have two scars and seeds have one scar.

Flowering plants have several mechanisms for dispersing fruits and seeds. These include wind, water, explosive mechanisms and special adaptations that encourage animals to disperse seeds.

Plants can photosynthesise

Plants are unique in that they make their own food. Using carbon dioxide and water they can build up or **synthesise** these relatively small substances into bigger substances provided there is sunlight as an energy source and a green pigment called **chlorophyll**. The chlorophyll traps the light energy and uses it to synthesise foods such as glucose. The process is represented by this word equation (**Figure 23**):

Asexual reproductive structures

Some plants store their surplus food in modified structures that help them reproduce asexually.

Potatoes are swollen underground stems or **tubers** of stored food.

Onions, daffodils and other **bulbs** store food at the base of leaves within the bulb. Such stores enable plants to begin growing early in the year, make maximum use of light, flower and make seeds before tree canopies develop. Crocus and other plants that make **corms** store food in modified stems. Each of these structures can grow into new plants without the need of pollination and fertilisation; they are products of asexual reproduction and are genetically identical to the parent plant.

Plants and water

Water carried up plant stems is eventually returned to the air in a process called **transpiration**. If food colouring is added to water in which a

Figure 23

Carbon dioxide + water + $\xrightarrow[\text{Chlorophyll}]{\text{Light}}$ Glucose + oxygen

This process is called **photosynthesis** and is vital for all life. Only plants with chlorophyll can make their own food. All animals ultimately depend on photosynthesis for food and the oxygen that is a bi-product of the process.

cut flower, e.g. carnation, is placed, the woody tubes through which the water moves become stained and can be easily seen with a lens. The process can be undertaken in half a day in a warm room. The flower will also change colour proving that the tubes that carry the water up the stem are linked to those in the flower. Transpiration delivers water to the leaves for use in photosynthesis.

Much water is lost from leaves via transpiration and this keeps the thin leaves cool during hot and breezy weather. Evaporation of water involves a change of state from liquid to gas. Evaporation always causes cooling.

Lesson focus: *Green plants as organisms*

Early Learning Goal: Knowledge and understanding of the world

KS1 NC Ref: *Sc1 2b, f; Sc2 3b*   **Year group:** *Reception*

Scheme of work unit: *1B – Growing plants*

Intended learning: for children to observe and know that a flowering plant has a root, stem, leaf and flower.

Resources
❖ Some flowering plants, such as pansies, busy lizzies, dandelions (check ASE *Be Safe!* for plants which are safe to use) and photographs.
❖ Coloured Playdough/Plasticine: cream/white, green, yellow, red.
❖ Paints: white, black, green, yellow, red, brushes; paper and easel.
❖ Labels (word + picture) for leaf, stem, roots and flower.
❖ Blu-tack.

Introduction: *Whole class session*
Using large plant photographs and living plants, discuss the parts of the plant. Point to the different parts asking children to name them. Ask questions phrased to assess if children know stem, leaf, root and flower. Teach these terms. Refer to some real plants and use the same questions to encourage children to use the correct language. Invite children to point to the part of the plant as you name it. Then point to the part and the children name the part.

Group or individual activities
❖ The children choose and observe a plant.
❖ Through careful observation they either create a model using Playdough or Plasticine or paint a large picture.
❖ The teacher interacts with children framing questions about colours, shape, size of roots, stem, leaf and flower.
❖ Then the teacher provides pre-prepared labels of the parts of the plant.
❖ The children Blu-tack them on the correct part of their model/painting.

Plenary session
The children share their models/pictures with the rest of the class. Other children are challenged to check if each model/picture has labels in the correct place. Models minus labels are then left on an interactive table for children to practise using the labels on other children's models/paintings.

Points for assessment
❖ Could the children observe and correctly name the roots, stem, leaf and flower?

Lesson focus: *Green plants as organisms*

KS1 NC Ref: *Sc1 2a–j; Sc2 3a*   **Year group:** *Y1/2*

Scheme of work unit: *1B – Growing plants*

Intended learning: for children to plan, carry out and communicate an investigation on plant growth needing water.

Resources
❖ Mustard seeds, pots, compost, plastic measuring cylinders.

Introduction: *Whole class session*
Children draw an annotated picture of what a plant needs to grow. These ideas are discussed and the teacher focuses on plants needing water. The teacher supports the children's plans for investigating: 'Do seeds need water to grow?' (using a published scheme such as the *Star Science Planning House*), Make children's ideas explicit by recording:

❖ the question to be investigated;
❖ how they will do it;
❖ what they will need;
❖ how they will make it a fair test.

Group or individual activities
❖ Children participate in planning the investigation.
❖ They decide to plant some seeds in 'dry compost' and some in 'wet compost'. 20ml of water are added to the wet compost each day, but none to the dry compost.
❖ To make the test fair, both pots are placed in the same sunny, warm place.
❖ Over three weeks children measure the height of the tallest plant using different coloured centicubes each week. They leave them on the pot. This creates a 3-D bar graph.
❖ The teacher also records the height of the tallest plant in a two-column table each week.

Plenary session
The teacher refers to the table s/he has prepared and relates it to the bar graph they have 'built'. S/he explains that the bar graph tells a story of what happened. S/he questions the children about these measurements. In which pot did the seeds grow? How was this pot different? Why did the seeds only grow in one of the pots? Do plants need water to grow?

Points for assessment
❖ Do the children know that plants need water to grow?
❖ Do they know the main features of an investigation?
❖ Do they need more support with planning?

Lesson focus: *Green plants as organisms*

KS2 NC Ref: *Sc1 2a–c, e–j, l; Sc2 3c*   **Year group:** *Y3/4*

Scheme of work unit: *3B – Helping plants grow well*

Intended learning: for children to know that water moves through a plant stem and into leaves and flowers; to investigate how quickly water moves through a stem.

Resources
❖ Cut plants, such as white carnations and daffodils.
❖ Red or blue food colouring.
❖ A range of timers.
❖ Plastic beakers.

Introduction: *Whole class session*
Revise the parts of the flowering plant. Ask the children where they think water goes in the plant. Explain that they are to find out the route water takes through the plant using cut flowers and food colouring. Challenge them to plan their own experiment making them report back to the class before proceeding. Children given an outline to record their findings:

Length of stem   cm

Time for dye to reach flower   min

Speed of movement = $\dfrac{\text{distance}}{\text{time}}$ = cm per minute

Pupil activity
Children add a few drops of food colouring to water. They choose a timer and commence measuring time as soon as the plant stem is placed in the dye. Every 30 minutes they observe their plant. Timing stops as soon as the dye reaches the flower. By measuring the length of the plant they can express the time it takes for the water to move through the stem. More able pupils could express this as speed, as shown:

$$\text{Speed (cm per minute)} = \frac{\text{Length of stem}}{\text{Time to reach flower}}$$

Under supervision they can cut through the middle of the stem and make an observational drawing with a magnifying glass. They should see the dyed tubes which carried dyed water. These tubes are called xylem. For a homework activity children are challenged to see if they can make the water travel up a plant stem more quickly, e.g. putting plants and dye in a warmer place.

Plenary session

Children explain how they measured how fast the dye moved. They describe their observational drawings and offer possible answers to the teacher's challenges. They explain that only the coloured parts in the stem carried the water because only these parts became coloured.

Points for assessment

❖ Do they know that water moves in special parts of the stem?
❖ Can they plan an experiment to find out how quickly water moves through a stem?
❖ Can they choose suitable timers for the experiment?
❖ Can they use equipment with teacher support?

Teacher's own notes:

Lesson focus: *Green plants as organisms*

KS2 NC Ref: *Sc1 1a, 2a–m; Sc2 3a, 3d*   **Year group:** *Y5/6*

Scheme of work unit: *5B – Life cycles*

Intended learning: to know that seeds will germinate if they have water; to plan, carry out and consider the evidence from an investigation; to recognise the importance of using many seeds to get reliable evidence.

Resources
❖ Bean seeds.
❖ Cotton wool.
❖ Plastic trays.
❖ Paper towels.
❖ Water.
❖ Planning board, frameworks.

Introduction: *Whole class session*
Explain that germination is when a seed starts to grow, producing a small root and shoot. Children are told that they will investigate how much water is needed for bean seeds to germinate. They should brainstorm their ideas. The teacher helps groups to make an idea into a question to investigate. The class decides that they use ten seeds in each test and will measure the number of days for roots to appear from five different seeds in the sample.

The partly completed planning board framework below is discussed to support planning.

Questions to investigate:

❖ What we will change;
❖ What we will judge or measure – number of days for five seeds to develop a root;
❖ What we will keep the same to make the test fair.

Group or individual activities
❖ The children plan their investigation and have it checked by the teacher.
❖ They then proceed with the investigation, deciding what to change and what to keep the same. (Some children decide to place ten seeds on a paper towel in each of four plastic trays. In the first tray they give no water. In the second tray, 10ml of water, in the third, 20ml of water and the fourth tray, 30ml of water. Each tray is covered with cling film to stop evaporation and placed in a warm, dark place.)
❖ The trays are observed daily. The results are recorded in a two-column table.
❖ The children make a graph of their results using a bar or stick graph.

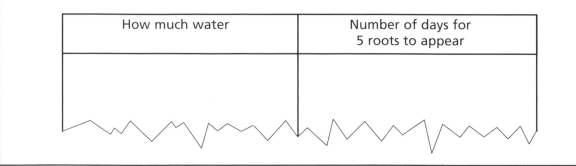

How much water	Number of days for 5 roots to appear

Plenary session

After the seeds have germinated each group presents its findings to the class. The teacher helps them to make the connection between germination and the need for warmth rather than light.

Points for assessment
❖ Do the children know what germination is?
❖ Can they plan an investigation deciding what to change?
❖ Do they recognise the need for using several seeds to obtain reliable evidence?

Teacher's own notes:

Chapter 2
Ourselves

Animals can be classified into two groups: **vertebrates** which have a backbone and **invertebrates**, e.g. snails, worms, insects, which have no backbone. Humans are vertebrates.

All animals carry out seven processes to stay alive and maintain continuity of life:

▲ breathing;
▲ feeding;
▲ growing;
▲ excreting;
▲ moving;
▲ responding to stimuli;
▲ reproducing.

Background knowledge of these processes is given below.

Breathing

Breathing is an exchange of gases. Oxygen is taken in and used for respiring food such as glucose. Every living cell has to respire to stay alive. **Respiration** releases energy that the animal needs for maintaining life activities such as moving, repairing and replacing cells. Carbon dioxide is a waste, poisonous product of respiration and is breathed out. This process is virtually the opposite of photo-synthesis because food and oxygen are used to make carbon dioxide and water and it releases energy for vital activities (**Figure 24**).

Figure 24

Glucose + oxygen ⟶ Carbon dioxide + water + energy

Most animals and certainly humans can only respire for very short periods of time without oxygen.

Feeding

Feeding is the process of obtaining a variety of food types that form a balanced diet. Humans need the foods shown in the table overleaf to maintain health.

Water makes up about 70 – 80% of human body mass and is vital for life processes.

Teeth and feeding

Teeth are used to obtain food and prepare it for digestion. There are different types and numbers of teeth and they perform different functions. The first set of teeth, called **milk teeth**, appears in the mouth from about six months of age. Adult teeth begin to appear from six years of age as the

Food types	Purpose
Carbohydrates, e.g. starch and sugars	To provide energy
Proteins, e.g. fish, meat, dairy products, pulses	To provide the raw materials for growth, i.e. for making new cells
Fats, e.g. butter, oils, margarine, dairy products	Essential for making cell membranes; provide energy stores; important for insulation in marine mammals, e.g. whales
Vitamins needed in regular, small amounts and found in dairy products, fruit, vegetables, fish liver oils	To maintain body health, e.g. for maintaining vision, bones, healthy skin and teeth
Minerals, e.g. dairy products, red meats, vegetables	To maintain body parts, e.g. iron for red blood cells, calcium for bones and teeth

Figure 25

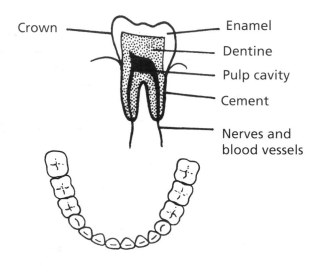

Crown — Enamel
— Dentine
— Pulp cavity
— Cement
— Nerves and blood vessels

mouth increases in size. The upper jaw in a complete dentition has the same number and type of teeth as the lower jaw. The right side of each jaw is symmetrical with the left-hand side.

The part of the tooth that projects above the gum is the **crown**. It is white and covered with **enamel** – the hardest substance in the body. Below the gum the root is fixed into the jawbone by a substance called **cement**. **Dentine** is a softer substance and is under the enamel bearing microscopic tubes that secrete enamel.

Type of tooth, shape, and position	Number in milk set	Number in adult set	Function
Incisor – front of mouth; chisel shaped	8	8	For biting food
Canine – behind the incisors; pointed	4	4	For tearing food
Premolars – behind the canines; flat top with 2 points	8	8	For grinding and crushing food
Molars – behind the premolars; flat crown with four points	8	12	For grinding, chewing and crushing food
Total	28	32	

The pulp cavity in the centre of the tooth has a blood and nerve supply. The crown of the tooth and the gums become coated with bacteria called **plaque**. Plaque acts upon waste foods, especially sugars, to make an acid that dissolves the enamel and dentine (**Figure 25**). Dental hygiene involving regular brushing of teeth and gums, reducing sugary food intake, and regular dental check ups help to prevent dental decay and gum disease.

Digestion follows feeding. Digestion involves changing the size of food particles so that they are small enough to pass through the gut wall. For example, **starch** is a large water-insoluble molecule made up of smaller glucose units that cannot pass through the gut wall. **Glucose** is water-soluble and can pass through the gut wall. In the body, digestive juices change large water-insoluble particles into smaller, water-soluble ones that can pass through the gut wall into the blood. Starch is digested to glucose; proteins to smaller constituents called **amino acids**; and fats digested to fatty acids and **glycerol**. Blood then transports them to all cells in the body.

Growing

All animals grow. Growth is an irreversible increase in size. All animals are made of cells and increasing the number of cells causes growth. There are about 100 billion cells in an adult human, each consisting of a cell membrane, a living jelly-like material called cytoplasm, and a nucleus. The nucleus contains chromosomes inherited from parents and controls all the activities in a cell. All cells in the human body, apart from sex cells, contain a copy of the 46 chromosomes inherited at fertilisation. The sex cells contain 23 chromosomes bearing genes that have been shuffled so that each sex cell is genetically different (**Figures 26** and **27**). Identical twins are derived from the same fertilised egg so have the same genetic information. Non-identical twins are formed from two different eggs and sperm cells and each has different genetic information.

Figure 26

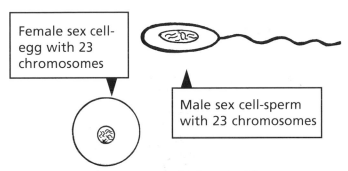

23 + 23 = 46 chromosomes in fertilised human egg

Tissues and organs

As they grow and develop, cells differentiate and undertake different functions. A collection of similar cells is a called a **tissue**, e.g. muscle tissue. A collection of different tissues is found in an **organ**, e.g. the skin has muscle tissue, fat tissue, blood tissue, etc, and is an example of an organ. A collection of different and essential organs, e.g. heart, gut, brain, skin, bone, kidneys, etc, forms an **organism**.

Humans grow until they have physically matured, i.e. when they have the optimum number of cells. Ageing begins when repair and replacement of body parts – tissues – is slower than the rate they wear out. Death occurs when all live processes cease.

Figure 27

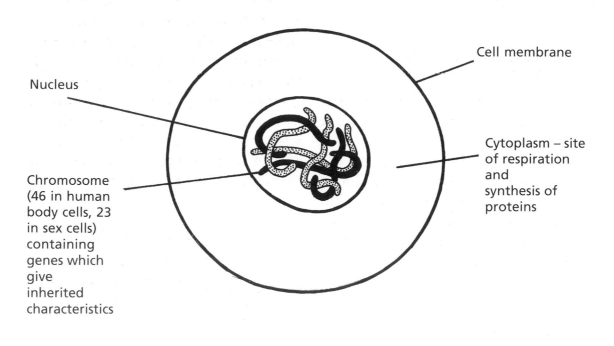

Nucleus

Cell membrane

Cytoplasm – site of respiration and synthesis of proteins

Chromosome (46 in human body cells, 23 in sex cells) containing genes which give inherited characteristics

Moving

All animals move. Movement is essential to avoid danger and for obtaining food. Animals move by walking, running, hopping, leaping, flying, swimming, crawling, flying, etc. Energy for movement comes from respiring digested foods. The human skeleton provides a framework for muscle attachment. Muscles are joined to bones by **tendons** and are found in pairs, each member working in opposition to the other. When muscles contract they move jointed bones by exerting a pulling force. For example, the arm is bent when the muscle on the front of the upper arm – the biceps – shortens to pull the radius bone in the lower arm up. As this happens the triceps muscle on the back of the arm relaxes. To straighten the arm the triceps muscle contracts to pull the ulna bone down, thereby straightening the arm (**Figure 28**).

Figure 28

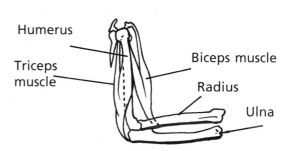

Humerus

Triceps muscle

Biceps muscle

Radius

Ulna

Other types of muscles, **not** attached to bones, are found in the heart, food canal, erector muscle of the hairs in the skin – those that cause goose pimples.

Excreting

This is the process whereby humans and other animals remove harmful waste products produced by their bodies. The lungs remove carbon dioxide, kidneys remove a toxic product of protein metabolism – urea – which is excreted as liquid urine. The skin also removes some urea and salts during sweating.

Responding to stimuli – sensitivity

Animals respond to changes in their surroundings. They have special sense organs that include sight, smell, taste, touch and hearing connected to the brain via a nervous system. These detectors of change in the environment cause changes in behaviour, e.g. the smell of fresh foods can cause 'mouth watering' in anticipation of eating them.

Reproducing

Animals must replace their kind if the species is to survive. Humans reproduce by sexual means that entail a male sex cell and a female sex cell joining in a process called fertilisation. A fertilised egg has a blueprint for development into a new life. The code is located in the nucleus in structures called chromosomes, and consists of a chemical called DNA. The shortest section of DNA that codes for a single characteristic is called a gene. For example, the gene for eye colour is inherited from parents at the point of fertilisation of an egg by a sperm. Humans have a huge number of genes. (See also unit on plants and growth.)

Blood and circulatory system

Blood is a medium that integrates different parts of the body. The table below shows the constituents and their functions.

Blood circulates around the body through **blood vessels**. A muscular pump called the **heart** pumps blood from the left-hand side of the heart into **arteries** that branch repeatedly to form into narrow **capillaries**. The capillaries

Constituent	Appearance	Function
Plasma	Straw coloured liquid	Transports: food such as glucose and amino acids, waste products, e.g. urea, carbon dioxide and heat
Red blood cells	▲ Circular biconcave discs with no nucleus ▲ Appear red in vast numbers ▲ Made in bone marrow of long bones	Transports oxygen to all cells in the body
White blood cells	Irregular in shape with a nucleus	Defence of body: feed upon bacteria and produce antibodies to destroy bacteria and viruses
Platelets	Very tiny and fewer in number than other blood cells	Help blood to clot

are very narrow with very thin walls and glucose, amino acids and oxygen leak into surrounding cells. Waste materials from cells move through the capillary walls into the blood. The capillaries lead to wider tubes called **veins** that converge into two large veins before returning to the right-hand side of the heart. Veins have valves to stop the back flow of blood.

The human heart is two pumps working in harmony. There are four chambers. The upper chambers are called **atria** and receive blood. When full they gently pump it into the main pumping chambers below; these are called **ventricles**. The right ventricle pumps blood to the lungs where carbon dioxide is exchanged for oxygen. This makes the blood bright red. A major vein carries blood to the left atria which pumps it to the ventricle below. The left ventricle is powerful enough to pump blood all round the body through arteries, capillaries and veins (**Figure 29**).

The heart beats approximately 72 times per minute at rest. The **pulse** of a resting person is found by placing a finger over an artery in the part of the wrist that is in line with the thumb. Each pulse is a surge of blood rushing through the artery as the heart pumps blood round the body. The heart rate needs to increase quickly during exercise to deliver extra oxygen and glucose to the muscles, and to take away the increased levels of carbon dioxide produced by increased rates of respiration. Pulse rate returns to normal a few minutes after exercise if a person is fit.

Figure 29

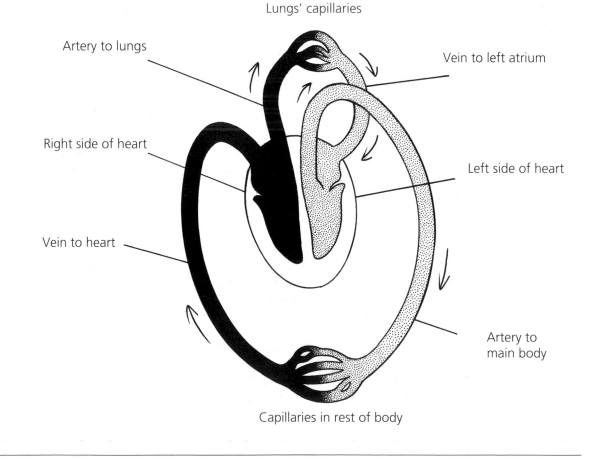

Lungs' capillaries

Artery to lungs

Vein to left atrium

Right side of heart

Left side of heart

Vein to heart

Artery to main body

Capillaries in rest of body

Lesson focus: *Animals and ourselves – body parts*

Early Learning Goal: *Knowledge and understanding of the world*

KS1 NC Ref: *Sc2 2a, 2b*   **Year group:** *Reception*

Scheme of work unit: *1A – Ourselves*

Intended learning: for children to know the names of some parts of the body, e.g. head, eye, elbow, knee, leg, arm, ankle, wrist, fingers, toes.

Resources
❖ Photographs of patients and carers in a hospital.
❖ X-ray photographs.
❖ Large sheets of paper.
❖ Felt-tipped pens.
❖ Labels – words and pictures – of body parts.
❖ Blu-tack.

Introduction: *Whole class session*
Stimulate the development of the role play/home corner into a hospital. Use photographs of a hospital to discuss why people are there and show X-ray photographs of what parts of our bodies are like 'inside'. To 'play' in a hospital it is useful to know body parts. Using a volunteer, ask one child to lie on a large piece of paper and draw round the child's body. Ask the children to name some parts of the body they know then give out pre-prepared labels of relevant parts bearing a symbolic picture. The children take turns to stick the labels onto the relevant place. (This supports the National Literacy Strategy for Reception – understanding print, word recognition, and vocabulary extension.)

Group or individual activities
❖ To reinforce the names of the main body parts, give the children either prepared A4 sheets with body outlines for them to draw and label additional parts, such as eyes, ears, mouth, or a jigsaw of body parts. Interact with the groups, focusing their attention on more detail such as: How many fingers on a hand? How many thumbs do you have?
❖ Using a large plastic mirror, get them to look in more detail at their own eyes: How many colours can you see? What shape are the coloured parts? How could you show the colours on your picture?

Plenary session
Share some of the work children have done, asking them to show the parts of the body pictures. Play 'Simon says'. Mount the large outline of the body at child height on the wall and put labels and Blu-tack in a box for pairs of children to practise adding the labels during the rest of the week.

Points for assessment
❖ Can the children label key parts of the body on their outlines?
❖ Can they talk about body parts on the jigsaw?
❖ Do they point to the correct parts of the body when playing 'Simon says'?

Lesson focus: *Animals and ourselves*

KS1 NC Ref: *Sc1 1, 2a, d–h, j; Sc2 1b, 2c*   **Year group:** *Y1/2*

Scheme of work unit: *2A – Health and growth*

Intended learning: for children to find out which flavour of crisp is the most popular by undertaking a class survey and communicating findings in a table and bar chart.

Resources
❖ Samples of different flavours of crisps (avoiding flavours that could be culturally offensive to any child). Alternatively, other foods could be offered from within a similar category, such as different fresh fruits, biscuits or cereals.
❖ Ready-prepared tables and graph outlines.

Introduction: *Whole class session*
Revise some of the foods that children eat at home and the ones that are healthy. Discuss how children could collect information about which type of crisp they prefer. Explain that each child will only taste one of each type of crisp, say, from four different flavours of the same brand to keep it fair. Then they will record just the type they prefer. Discuss the importance of recording findings and introduce a two-column table as a means of the teacher co-ordinating the recording of all the class data.

Group or individual activities

Type of crisp	Number of votes
Plain	*13*
Salt & vinegar	
Cheese & onion	
Chicken	

❖ The children taste up to four different types of crisp. Organise this so that the order of tasting is written on the table before tasting starts. (NB this a planning strategy.) The children then individually decide which one they will vote for. Co-ordinate the collection of votes and record the scores in a two-column table.
❖ Using this data, explain and show how the children's own survey can be shown as either a pictogram or bar graph. Ask for volunteers to help draw the bar graph.

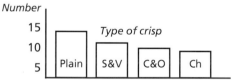

Plenary session
Ask the children to try and tell the story of the survey by talking about the graph. Ask questions to see if they can make sense of the survey, starting with easy questions and making them progressively more difficult. For example:

❖ How many types of crisp did we taste?
❖ Which was the most popular flavour?
❖ Which was the least popular flavour?
❖ How many more children preferred plain crisps to chicken crisps?
❖ What advice can the children offer to the school tuck shop following this survey?

Discuss whether a diet of crisps would be healthy, making connections to the importance of eating a variety of healthy foods other than snacks.

Points for assessment
❖ Do the children understand how the survey was carried out?
❖ Can they record in a table?
❖ Can they interpret the bar graph?

Lesson focus: *Animals and ourselves*

KS2 NC Ref: *Sc2, 2a*   **Year group:** *Y3/4*

Scheme of work unit: *3A – Teeth and eating*

Intended learning: for children to know that humans have four different kinds of teeth and that each type of tooth has a special job/function.

Resources
❖ Samples of sterilised human teeth or plastic models.
❖ Sterilised plastic mirrors.
❖ Model of jaw with teeth.
❖ Information books about teeth.

Introduction: *Whole class session*
Elicit children's ideas about why they need teeth; what teeth are like; and what teeth are for. Give five minutes for drawing and writing their ideas. Discuss these ideas as a class, then explain how ideas can be checked by careful observation and by using information in books.

Group or individual activities
❖ Ask the children to observe their teeth using a clean mirror. How are some teeth different? How many different shapes of teeth can they see? Are there any gaps? Have some teeth been repaired/filled? Why? What can they do to help prevent tooth decay? Discuss these observations, then ask them to listen and interact to questions as you explain about the types and functions of teeth using visual aids, samples of sterilised teeth and/or models of teeth.

Type of tooth	Feature: position/shape	Function: job
	Front	Biting food
Canine		
		Chewing
Molar		

❖ Children undertake a science literacy task to either consolidate or restructure any misconceptions and to extend their vocabulary of science terms by scanning information. Provide a suitable text, such as *Star Science: Ourselves and Other Animals* lower junior page 22 to scan, extract and record information about types of teeth to add to a partially completed table.

Plenary session
Ask the children to share their answers using the table they have completed and correct any errors. Emphasise the need to care for teeth and set a diary task for **homework** for them to record each day over the next week:

❖ when they clean their teeth;
❖ when and how many sweets they eat;
❖ when and if they visit the dentist.

Day	When teeth cleaned	Sweets: when/ how many?	Visit to the dentist?
Monday			

This will be discussed in the next science lesson.

Points for assessment
❖ Do the children know that there are four types of human teeth?
❖ Do they know where they are in the mouth, what shape each type is and what job it does?
❖ What do they know about care of teeth?

Lesson focus: *Animals and ourselves*

KS2 NC Ref: *Sc1 2a–m; Sc2 2e*   **Year group:** *Y5/6*

Scheme of work unit: *5A – Keeping healthy*

Intended learning: to plan and communicate an investigation into how pulse rate changes with increase in exercise and use science knowledge about the heart to explain findings.

Resources
❖ A range of timers for children to choose from appropriately.
❖ Graph paper.

Introduction: *Whole class session*
Revise the function of the heart. Explain that the pulse rate indicates how hard the heart works. Teach children how to take their pulse correctly (by placing fingers, not thumbs, over a bone in the wrist which is in line with the thumb and where an artery is close to the skin). Let them practise finding it. Explain that each pulse represents a heart beat and is expressed in beats per minute (it may be easier to take it for 30 seconds and double it). Ask for ideas about what to investigate about pulse rate. Turn their ideas into questions to investigate, such as: How does the length of exercise affect pulse rate? In this investigation, children will change the length of exercise between taking pulse rate, record the pulse rate after the exercise (to answer the question) and keep the type and duration of exercise (and child whose pulse is being investigated) the same, to make the test fair.

Discuss the need for reliable data. Will one measurement at rest be reliable? How can we make results more reliable? Consider the need for taking repeat readings and organising answers in tables which structure the recording of repeat readings and the finding of the mean. Taking three readings should improve reliability. Help all groups to decide to use the same type of exercise so that group results can be discussed more meaningfully when shared with the whole class.

Group or individual activities
In small groups, the children finalise plans for the investigation and design a suitable table. They choose equipment and then undertake the activity. Each group calculates the results and draws a line graph, on poster paper, for sharing with the whole class.

Plenary session
Each group presents its results. Help them to look for patterns in different groups' results and consider if generalisations can be made. Having established the pattern that pulse rate increases with exercise helps the children make the connection to the fact that exercise needs energy and to release energy muscles need more food and oxygen. By increasing the pulse rate, muscles get the raw materials they need to enable the extra exercise to take place. To reinforce learning and for homework, issue some secondary data of a very fit child athlete's pulse rate. They should graph the data and then raise a set of questions about the data for other children to answer.

Points for assessment
❖ Can the children plan an investigation?
❖ Can they design a table suitable for repeat readings and finding a mean value?
❖ Do they know and understand the reason why exercise increases pulse rate?

Chapter 3
Light

Light is emitted in waves from very hot sources such as the Sun, stars, fires, etc. It is a form of **energy** that is moving from a very hot source. It does not need any material medium as a transmitting agent and can travel through a vacuum such as outer space at 300,000km which is faster than anything else. **White light**, which we use to see objects, is the visible part of the electromagnetic spectrum that travels to Earth from the Sun. Other components of the electromagnetic spectrum are **gamma rays**, **X-rays**, **infra-red waves**, **ultra-violet rays**, **microwaves** and **radio-waves**.

White light is composed of seven colours – red, orange, yellow, green, blue, indigo and violet – the colours of the rainbow. Human eyes only detect the visible white light part of the electromagnetic spectrum. We cannot actually see light. We see light that has been 'bounced off' or 'reflected from' a surface. Light beams of Sun rays are reflected from dust particles in the air and we then see them.

When light reaches an object or surface, it can either be absorbed or reflected or partially absorbed and partially reflected. It is the light that is reflected into our eyes that we see.

Many children think that light comes from their eyes like a torch, i.e. that they have active vision and this is an idea that requires further probing and challenging by the teacher. If there is no light, or very little light, children will have difficulty seeing objects because light is not entering the eye.

Light travels in straight lines from its source. It can pass through **transparent** and **translucent** materials, but not through **opaque** materials. Opaque things block light and create shadows. Light bounces off opaque materials that scatter the light in all directions. Transparent materials, such as glass, let light through in straight lines and we can see the object through the glass. Crumpled aluminium foil does not produce a clear image of an observer because light is **scattered** in several directions.

Translucent materials such as greaseproof paper, bubble wrap or distorted bathroom glass let light through but deflect or scatter it in many directions so an image cannot be seen.

Shadows

Whenever an object blocks light, a shadow forms. Light passes by the edge of the object and a dark shape appears behind it where the light sources cannot reach (**Figure 30**). The shadow is the same shape as the object, but its size may vary depending on the angle at which the light hits the object. If the light comes from a steep angle above the object, a short shadow is cast; if the angle is small, a long shadow is cast. This effect is noticeable at early morning, noon and late evening on sunny days.

Shadows become smaller if the light source is moved away from the object used to create the shadow.

Figure 30

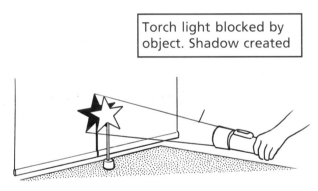

Torch light blocked by object. Shadow created

Reflection

Many surfaces reflect light, but flat shiny surfaces such as mirrors reflect light better than other types of surfaces so that an image can be seen. When light is shone at a mirror, light is reflected and demonstrates the law of reflection which states that the angle of incidence equals the angle of reflection (**Figure 31**).

Bending or refracting light

Light is bent or **refracted** when it passes from one medium into another, e.g. when light moves from air to glass it is bent because the speed at which it is travelling slows down and its direction changes.

How we see objects

When light enters the eye it travels in straight lines towards the outer transparent curved **cornea**. It is refracted towards the lens that also refracts the light before it passes through the transparent jelly-like vitreous humour which gives the eye its spherical shape. The light forms an inverted (upside down) image on the **retina**. The retina is light sensitive and has cells that detect colour – the **cones** – and **rod cells** that detect black or white. Rods and cones are connected by the optic nerve to the brain which interprets the image as being upright as well as the colour details. Cone cells are of three types: red, green and blue

Figure 31

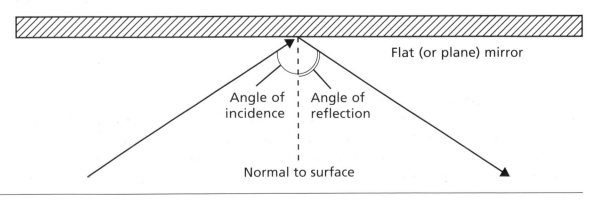

Flat (or plane) mirror

Angle of incidence

Angle of reflection

Normal to surface

colour cones. They enable humans to distinguish colours. Deficiency in one or more of the three colours of cones causes colour blindness.

The amount of light entering the eye is controlled by the coloured part – the **iris** – that surrounds the 'hole' or **pupil**. The pupil looks black but there is only transparent fluid there. As the size of the iris changes automatically according to light conditions, the pupil becomes smaller in bright conditions as the iris becomes larger. The converse occurs in dark conditions.

Figure 34

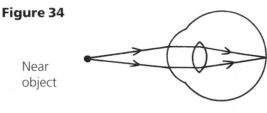

Near object

Spectacles are worn to correct defects caused when the lens does not adjust adequately to focus light on the retina.

Colour

Objects can reflect and absorb different wavelengths of light. Different colours bend differently when they pass

Figure 32

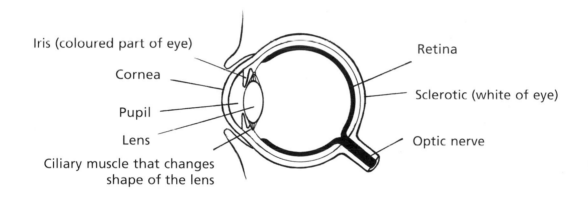

Iris (coloured part of eye)

Cornea

Pupil

Lens

Ciliary muscle that changes shape of the lens

Retina

Sclerotic (white of eye)

Optic nerve

The **ciliary muscles** change the shape of the lens to focus the image on the retina (**Figure 32**).

Figure 33

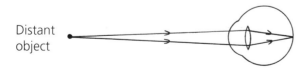

Distant object

The lens is long and thin when light from a distant object is focused on the retina. For light from a near object to be focused on the retina, the lens becomes shorter and fatter (**Figures 33** and **34**).

through transparent materials, e.g. when light passes through a glass prism to produce a spectrum of the colours of a rainbow (colour sequence in a spectrum is: red, orange, yellow, green, blue, indigo and violet). The red light bends least and the violet bends most (**Figurer 35**).

Remember! violet bends most violently.

When light shines through a coloured filter, e.g. a red acetate sheet, all the colours of the spectrum are absorbed except for red which is transmitted.

Figure 35

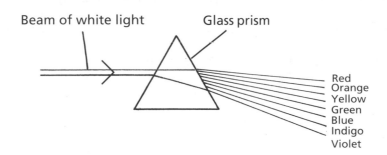

Beam of white light   Glass prism

Red
Orange
Yellow
Green
Blue
Indigo
Violet

Figure 36

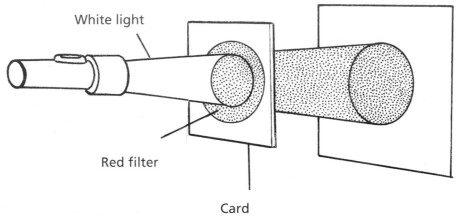

White light

Only red light
passes through.
Other colours
absorbed by
filter

Red filter

Card

Hence things look red when we look through red filters (**Figure 36**).

If we look at a red jumper, it looks red because the red light is reflected and the other colours are absorbed. White objects **reflect** all the colours and black objects **absorb** all the colours in white light. The sky appears to be blue because blue light is scattered down to the Earth more than red light. Sunsets appear to be red because when the sun is low in the sky, more red light gets through the air, whereas a lot of the blue light gets scattered so we do not see blue sunsets.

Lesson focus: *Light*

Early Learning Goal: *Knowledge and understanding of the world*

KS1 NC Ref: *Sc1 2a–c, f, g, j; Sc4 3b*   **Year group:** *Reception*

Scheme of work unit: *1D – Light and dark*

Intended learning: for children to know that light is needed to see things.

Resources
❖ A story or poem about light and dark, e.g. *The owl that was afraid of the dark*.
❖ Pictures of day and night scenes, e.g. *Star Science* (Ginn) *Big Book* p20.
❖ Old dark/black curtains and a table to make a very dark place.
❖ Ten different shapes of reflective strips.
❖ Two sheets of paper – one blue, one white – of outline drawings of shapes of reflective strips.
❖ Torch.
❖ One-minute sand timer.

Introduction: *Whole class session*
Discuss children's experience of day and night and how they are different. Use large pictures of the same scene in day and night. Read a story about night. Discuss when it is easy and hard to see. Set the group a task. The role-play area has been made into a dark place using dark curtains and a table. Hidden in the dark place are shapes (e.g. stars, letters, animals) made from reflective strips. These need finding and matching and recording to either the blue (for dark) or white (for torch) template sheet.

Group or individual activities
Children work in groups of four.

❖ Two children go into the dark place without a torch to try to find shapes and two children use the one-minute sand timer to tell them when to stop searching.
❖ After one minute they leave the dark with the shapes found and match them to the outline drawings on the blue sheet. They record their findings by ticking and counting.
❖ The children who timed the task then hide the shapes for the other pair to find, this time using a torch.
❖ After a timed minute they match the shapes collected to the white template sheet and record and count them again. The pairs swap roles and repeat the activity.

Plenary session
Encourage the children to share their findings, asking questions such as:

❖ When was it hard to find the shapes?
❖ When was it easy?
❖ How did they know it was easier to find the shapes using the torch? (Hint for helping children consider evidence: count the outline shapes 'ticked' for dark – the blue sheet, and then repeat for the shapes found using the torch.)
❖ Why was it hard to find the shapes in the dark? (Answer – because there was no light.)
❖ What do we need to be able to see?

Points for assessment
❖ Could the children record their findings?
❖ Did they use their findings, with teacher support, to reason that we need light to see?

Lesson Focus: *Light*

KS1 NC Ref: *Sc1 1, 2a–j; Sc4 3a*   **Year group:** *Y1/2*

Scheme of work unit: *1D – Light and dark*

Intended learning: to know that there are many sources of light and that light is only given out when things get very hot. To plan, carry out and communicate an investigation with teacher support.

Resources
❖ Candles.
❖ Sparklers – two different brands.
❖ Pictures of light sources and Bonfire Night, *Star Science* (Ginn) *Big Book* planning house.

Introduction: *Whole class session*
Ask the children to draw pictures of things that give out or make light. Share their ideas. Extend this range by considering sources of light in the classroom – computers, warning lights on switches. Challenge children to look for and draw or collect pictures of light sources to add to a collage over the next few weeks. Ask them to think about why some things give off light. Seasonal festivals, celebrations such as Diwali, Halloween, Bonfire Night and Christmas provide useful contexts. Use a picture of a bonfire scene. What things give out light? Why? Make the connection between heat and light.

Group or individual activities
Safety! This practical activity will need adult supervision.

❖ Show two packets of different brands of sparklers (or you could use candles). Show them to the group. Compare them – how are they alike, how are they different?
❖ Why are they not giving out light? How could we make them give out light? Consider this and the safety code for using fireworks.
❖ Help the children plan how to find out which was the best sparkler. Use a planning house to help them focus on the key points, especially things they could use to judge the quality of each sparkler (the brightness, how long it burned for, the colour of light emitted, how to make the test fair).
❖ Encourage them to predict which one will be best, then go into a safe place, e.g. the playground, and carry out the test. An adult should light each sparkler in turn and hold it away from the children, in a gloved hand, throughout. Children time how long each sparkler burns and the teacher co-ordinates a group vote based on the criteria for what has been deemed to mean 'best'. The teacher could record the summarised vote in a table.

Brand of sparkler	Score
Sainco	☆ ☆ ☆ ☆
Burystand	☆ ☆

Plenary session

Co-ordinate a review of the findings by asking questions such as:

- ❖ What did we do to make the test fair?
- ❖ Which sparkler burnt for the longest time?
- ❖ How much longer did it burn?
- ❖ Why were the sparklers easy to see when burning? (Answer: they gave off light when they were very hot and burning.)
- ❖ Which was judged the best? How do our class results tell us this? (Focus: can they use the table of results with teacher support to answer this?)
- ❖ Was the test fair? (Check: Were the sparklers observed from the same distance each time? Was the timer started and stopped at the right point in the procedure? Was it fair to compare results on information collected?)
- ❖ Why was this sparkler the best?

Children make a cartoon sequence of the investigation and write some sentences to summarise the findings.

Points for assessment

- ❖ Could the children understand how to plan the investigation?
- ❖ Could they plan and use the evidence, with teacher support, to reach a conclusion?
- ❖ Do they know an adequate range of things which give out light?
- ❖ Do they know that very hot things give out light?

Teacher's own notes:

Lesson focus: *Light*

KS2 NC Ref: *Sc4 3b*   **Year group:** *Y3/4*

Scheme of work unit: *3F – Light and shadows*

Intended learning: for children to know that shadows are formed when light is blocked by objects.

Resources
❖ Dowel.
❖ Card.
❖ Blu-tack.
❖ Torch.
❖ OHP.

Introduction: *Whole class session*
Ask children what shadows are and where they have seen them. Find out their ideas about how shadows are formed. Refine or reinforce the fact that if light from a source is blocked then a shadow is formed. Demonstrate this using, for example, a comb and bright torch projecting the shadow onto a screen or white background. Focus on how the shadow is formed: the plastic teeth block the light and appear black – the shadow – and the gaps where the light passes through are white.

Group or individual activities
Safety! This practical activity will need adult supervision.

❖ Children collect some objects that let light through and some that do not. You could introduce the terms 'transparent' and 'opaque'.
❖ They make a record of the shadows by drawing around them. They should note that only opaque objects make shadows.
❖ To extend and apply this idea, challenge them to make a set of shadow stick puppets to 'act' a nursery rhyme or a story for children in Reception. Shadow stick puppets are made using dowelling to which card shapes are fixed. For example, drain pipe, Sun, cloud/rain and spider shapes could be used to act out the nursery rhyme *Incey Wincey Spider* as a shadow puppet play. A powerful torch in a dim part of the room should produce shadows. The most effective shadows are made using an overhead projector but this should be supervised by an adult.

Plenary session
Let each group make presentations of their shadow puppet plays. They should explain how they created the shadow effects. Challenge them to make their shadows bigger or smaller, and generalise the rule for this procedure. Children record how shadows are made and how their size can be changed. The successful puppet plays could be presented to a Reception class or in assembly and children could explain how the shadow puppets work.

Points for assessment
❖ Could they make shadows?
❖ Do the children know how a shadow is made?
❖ Do they know the meaning of opaque and transparent?

Lesson focus: *Light*

KS2 NC Ref: *Sc4 3d*   **Year group:** *Y5/6*

Scheme of work unit: *6F – How we see things*

Intended learning: for children to know that we see objects when the object reflects light which enters our eyes.

Resources
❖ Paper tail.
❖ Blu-tack.
❖ Candle and matches.
❖ Plastic mirrors.
❖ Blindfold.

Introduction: *Whole class session*
Draw a large donkey minus its tail on the board. Prepare a tail for it and play the blindfold game 'fixing the tail on the donkey'. Discuss why it is difficult to place the tail correctly, focusing on the key idea previously taught (KS1) that we need light to be able to see. Ask the children to think about how we see things. Now light a candle.

Group or individual activities
The children draw and write their ideas to explain how they see the burning candle. They draw lines with arrows to show the direction in which light travels. (Note: many children think that light travels from the eye to the object and back again. This is a misconception. We can only see things when light enters our eyes from an object[1]. In this case some light from a candle flame travels into our eye and we can then see it. If a blindfold is worn when the candle is lit, the flame cannot be seen.)

❖ Children could now observe their own eye, carefully using a plastic mirror, and then draw a large diagram of their eye. Explain that the black part in the middle of the eye – the pupil – is a hole that lets light into the back of the eye.
❖ Challenge them to cover up their eyes for 30 seconds and when they open them again to observe their pupil in the mirror immediately. The pupil should be wide open in the dark but when light reaches it again it becomes smaller to control the amount of light entering the eye. Ask a friend to close their eyes. As they open them, watch the pupils respond to the light.

[1] Reflected light is needed – unless the object is itself a light source, such as the candle.

Plenary session
Children share their drawings of how they saw the candle. Discuss the direction of the arrows on the lines they have drawn to represent light. They should be in the direction of the eye. Ask them to explain how light enters the eye. Challenge them to create a different game from the Donkey's Tail which would also show that we see things when light enters our eye, e.g. building a Lego model blindfolded under time constraints.

For homework, research and list some occupations in which 'extra' light is needed to enable the person to see really well (dentist, surgeon, jeweller, etc).

Points for assessment

❖ Do children know that we see objects because light from them is reflected into our eyes?
❖ Can they represent how light travels from objects using lines with arrow heads pointing in the correct direction?

Teacher's own notes:

Chapter 4
Sound

Sound is a form of energy. It is different from light in that it requires a medium – a solid, liquid or gas – to travel through. Objects only make sound when they move. They need an input of energy to move. Movements that cause sound are called vibrations. A vibration is one backward and forward movement. This can be illustrated if a long section of a metre ruler is 'twanged' or vibrated on a desk (**Figure 37**).

How do vibrations cause sound?

A **vibrating** object causes the particles in the surrounding medium – air, liquid or solid – to move. For example, if a hand bell is rung in a playground, the air particles adjacent to the vibrating bell become squashed or **compressed**, whereas the air next to the 'first bit of compressed air' is less squashed or **decompressed**.

Figure 37

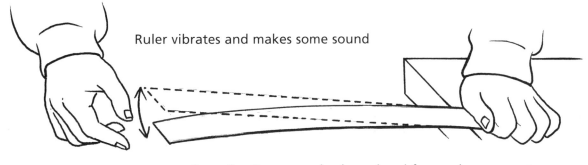

Ruler vibrates and makes some sound

One vibration = one backward and forward movement

The longer the section of ruler that vibrates, the longer the time for one vibration. Long lengths of ruler create lower sounds and it is easier to see the backward and forward movements. The shorter the section of ruler that vibrates, the higher the sound and the number of backward and forward movements per second is greater, so the movement looks blurred.

Decompression is also called a **rarefaction**. As the sound travels away from the source, the zone that was initially compressed becomes decompressed and the decompressed zone becomes compressed.

The sound travels outwards from its source in all directions in waves creating alternate zones of compressions of

Figure 38

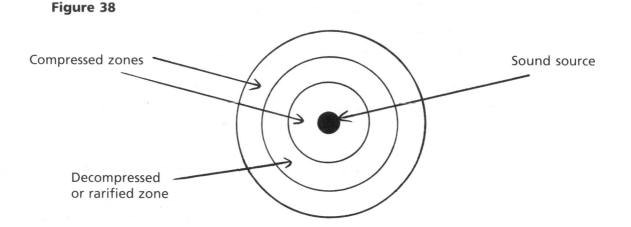

Compressed zones

Sound source

Decompressed or rarified zone

higher air pressure and rarefactions of lower air pressure (**Figure 38**). The number of vibrations in a second is the **frequency** of the sound. Frequency determines what the sound is like. In music, middle C has a frequency of 256 vibrations per second and this is now written as 256 Hertz (Hz). Sounds with high frequencies have a high **pitch** and those with a lower frequency have a lower pitched sound. High and low sounds or notes refer to pitch, not to the loudness of the sound.

length or thickness of the string, a lower pitched note is produced. Similarly, when air vibrates in organ pipes, it is the short columns of air that produce high-pitched notes whereas the long columns make lower pitched notes (**Figure 39**). The loudness depends on the amount of energy carried by the sound. A big hit on a drum skin makes a louder noise than a gentle hit, so we can make sounds that are loud or soft yet of the same pitch. The amount of energy

Figure 39

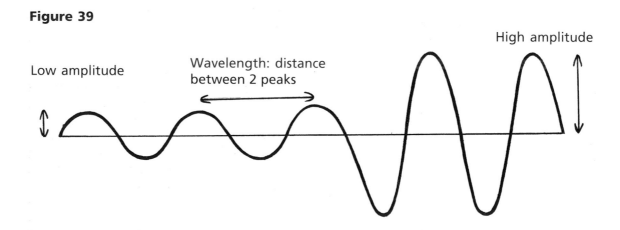

Low amplitude

Wavelength: distance between 2 peaks

High amplitude

Amplitude is a measure of how **loud** a particular sound is, varying the length or quantity of material that is made to vibrate changes the pitch. When a short length of string is made to vibrate on a violin or guitar, a high pitched note is made. By increasing either the

determines the amplitude.

Sound travels faster through solids and liquids than it does through air. In air, sound travels at about 330 metres per second which is much slower than the speed of light. That is why we see lightning before we hear the thunder.

In water it travels at about 1,400 metres per second. Sound can also bounce off surfaces in a similar way to light reflection. Bats navigate their flight by using **sonar** which depends on reflected sound. A reflected sound wave can give a second sound or **echo** of the first sound. Fabrics such as curtains and carpets absorb sound and reduce echoes whereas smooth and hard surfaces encourage echoes.

Figure 40

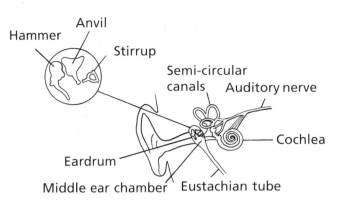

The ear and hearing

The ear is the organ responsible for detecting sound.

The ear has three main parts: the outer ear, middle ear and inner ear. Each part has special structures which determine the functions they perform (**Figure 40**).

Children need to develop the idea that sounds are produced, transmitted and received. They find it difficult to understand how we hear sounds, frequently saying 'by listening'. This may imply an active mode of receiving sound.

Part	Feature and location	Function
Outer ear	The earlobe, and tube leading to ear drum. Lobe is curved, ear canal leads to the ear drum	To collect sound, reflect it into the ear canal and channel the sound to the ear drum
Middle ear	Ear drum and air-filled chamber bearing three small bones, which are connected to an oval membrane	Ear drum vibrates and this causes sound to be transmitted through three small bones to the oval window. Eustachian tube enables air pressure to be equal on both sides of the ear drum. Blockage of the Eustachian tube by catarrh can cause earache as the air pressure on each of the ear drums may not be equal
Inner ear	Chamber is connected to back of throat by a eustachian tube. Contains a coiled, hollow shell-like bone, the cochlea, that is fluid-filled and has sensitive nerve cells that connect to the brain	When the oval window vibrates it causes fluid in the cochlea to vibrate. Different frequencies of sound are detected by different sets of nerve cells. The nerve cells send electrical messages to the brain which interprets and differentiates between different types of sound and the direction from which it came

Lesson focus: *Sound*

Early Learning Goals: *Knowledge and understanding of the world; Creative development*

KS1 NC Ref: *Sc1 1 2a, b, f–h; Sc4 3c*   **Year group:** *Reception*

Scheme of work unit: *1F – Sound and hearing*

Intended learning: for children to know that there are many kinds of sounds and to explore making a range of sounds to accompany a story or role play.

Resources
❖ Story books, e.g. *Jack and the Beanstalk*, *Billy Goats Gruff*.
❖ Drum, chime bars, dowel, metal tray, metal spoon, plastic spoon, bells, blocks of wood, xylophone, recorder, coconut shells, cymbals.

Introduction: *Whole class session*
Ask the children to listen very quietly for one minute (use a sand timer) to sounds they can hear in the classroom. Discuss the sounds and list those heard collectively by the class. Develop them as flash cards for a language board. Read a poem such as *Ride A Cock Horse* or *Old King Cole*, which has sounds in it. Ask children how these noises in the poem could be made using things in the classroom. Let some children try it and show the class their ideas.

Group or individual activities
Challenge the groups to find ways of making sounds to accompany a story that the teacher will read later to the whole class. Share the key points of the story with the group and discuss what sounds might be like, for example loud, quiet, high, low, pleasant, unpleasant. Each group then explores the available sound making equipment to decide the best sounds to use for different parts of the story.

Plenary session
Choose a group to provide the sounds as you read the story to the class, giving the group relevant cues as necessary. Pause after each sound to discuss its qualities and develop language such as 'loud', 'quiet', 'noise', 'pleasant', 'unpleasant', 'high' and 'low'. (These could be prepared as flash cards to use as the discussion merits and then displayed on a language board.) Alternatively this language could be discussed and developed at the end of the story. Finally, set a challenge for groups to role play a story of an accident. What sounds would be made for an ambulance or police car, telephone, fast car, skidding car, and so on? Let them present their role play with sounds at another time and add any relevant new words to the class list of sound words.

Points for assessment
❖ Can the children name some sounds heard in the classroom?
❖ Can they make different sounds for the story and role play?
❖ Can they use language accurately to describe some different sounds?

Lesson focus: *Sound*

KS1 NC Ref: *Sc1 1; 2a–j; Sc4 3d*   **Year group:** *Y1/2*

Scheme of work unit: *1F – Sound and hearing*

Intended learning: for children to carry out an investigation into how sounds become fainter the further they travel from a source.

Resources
❖ Drum or triangle and bar.
❖ Plasticine, card, dowel.
❖ Table to record results.
❖ Picture of scene with 'noisy elements', e.g. airport or railway station.
❖ Recording of plane or train moving towards and away from a person.
❖ Tape recorder.
❖ Outline of table.

Introduction: *Whole class session*
Revise with children how sounds are made and how our ears help us to hear. Display a picture, for example, of an airport or railway station. Ask them what sounds would be like here. List them. Now ask the children to explain how the sounds from moving things (aeroplane, train) change as they approach you. Check their ideas by playing a relevant tape recording. Can they tell when the vehicle is coming towards them and moving away from them? What happens to the sound when the vehicle is moving away? Then support the children in planning their own investigation 'to find out if sounds get fainter the further away a person is from the sound'. Help them to plan a fair test and decide how they will record how loud the sound is at three different distances from its source. Using sound flags made from card and dowel with phrases such as 'very loud', 'loud', 'quiet', they are to count and record the number of steps away from the sound source. Show them how to record this in a table.

Group or individual activities
Children participate in groups in the playground. One child stays in the same place (e.g. middle of playground) and plays the same sound with a drum or triangle all the time for the groups to hear. Each group decides how loud it is where they are standing and mark it with the 'right' sound flag. Then children walk to or from the sound, 'flagging' the sound appropriately until they have used the three flag markers. To ensure a fair test only one child in each group counts the number of steps from the source to each flag. This is recorded in the table.

Plenary session
Co-ordinate the group results by using a large prepared table. Ask them what they notice about the sound when it is near the source and when it is further away from it. Explain that all the groups have found a similar pattern (if this is the case) and make a link to the sound of the moving vehicle on the tape recorder. Ask the children to look back to the title of the investigation and ask them if their results and the other groups' results give an answer to it.

Points for assessment
❖ Do the children know that sounds get fainter the further away a person is from the source?
❖ Can they record in a table?
❖ Do they draw on their knowledge of sound to explain the results in the table?

Lesson focus: *Sound*

KS2 NC Ref: *Sc1 2d, h, i; Sc4 3e*   **Year group:** *Y3/4*

Scheme of work unit: *5F – Changing sounds*

Intended learning: for children to know that a sound is made when an object vibrates.

Resources
- ❖ Tuning fork.
- ❖ Table to record results.
- ❖ Rice.
- ❖ Plastic petri dish.
- ❖ Metre stick.
- ❖ Elastic bands.
- ❖ Table tennis ball.
- ❖ String and Sellotape.
- ❖ Drum and stick.
- ❖ OHP
- ❖ Plastic box.

Introduction: *Whole class session*
Elicit children's ideas about how sounds are made by asking them to draw and write their ideas. Review their findings. They may not be aware of what a vibration is. Demonstrate this. Use a table tennis ball suspended on 30cm of thread/string. Strike a tuning fork on an old cork. Ask the children to listen to it as you hold it vertically in the air. While it is still sounding, move the fork towards the suspended table tennis ball so that a prong just touches it. The vibrating prong will make the ball move away from the fork. Try and play 'ping pong' with the vibrating fork. The ball will continue to swing to and fro using the energy that has been transferred to it from the tuning fork. One backwards and forwards movement is a vibration. This illustrates that when something emits a sound it vibrates but we cannot always see the vibrations. The faster something vibrates in a second, the higher the pitch of the sound and vice versa. Now demonstrate how a tuning fork causes ripples in water.

Safety! Adult supervision for this.

Place some water in a transparent petri dish. Place it on an OHP. Sound the fork and place a prong on the water surface carefully. Note that some water beads 'jump' out of the dish on to the OHP surface. The OHP magnifies this effect for all to see. Let a child sound the tuning fork and carefully place it on the back his or her hand. S/he should feel the tingling caused by the moving prongs even though the vibrations are not easily seen.

Group or individual activities
- ❖ Provide a range of activities for children to experience vibrations: twanging a ruler from the edge of a table. How can they make the sound change?
- ❖ Place rice grains on the surface of a drum and hit it. What makes the rice move? As the drum skin vibrates it moves the rice and makes a sound.
- ❖ Place elastic bands across plastic containers. Pluck them. Can children see the vibrations? Can they hear the sounds? What causes the sound?

Experiment	Observation	Causes of sound
Tuning fork and ball		
Twanging ruler		
Rice on drum		
Elastic band		

The children record these activities systematically by drawing and writing in a worksheet.

Plenary session

The children share their findings with the class. They are challenged to describe what made each object vibrate, what they could observe that supported the concept of a vibration, and how sounds are made. Some different objects, e.g. bell, triangle and guitar, are presented and the class discusses what vibrates from each to cause sound.

Points for assessment

❖ Do the children know what a vibration is?
❖ Can they see and feel vibrations when some things make sound?
❖ Do they know that vibrations cause sounds?

Teacher's own notes:

Lesson focus: *Sound*

KS2 NC Ref: *Sc1 1, 2a–m; Sc4 3g*　　　　　　**Year group:** *Y5/6*

Scheme of work unit: *5F – Changing sounds*

Intended learning: for children to know some materials which can muffle sound; to plan, carry out, and consider evidence from an investigation.

Resources
❖ Stop clock or other object that makes sound such as a transistor radio or tape recorder.
❖ Cardboard box.
❖ Either a sound meter (portable), computer or sound sensor to link to a computer (e.g. *First Sense*, *Ecolog*).
❖ A range of insulating material, e.g. bubble wrap, newspaper, curtain fabric, polystyrene and carpet.

Introduction: *Whole class session*
Discuss with children the issue of noise as a pollutant. Why is it that in some parts of the school it seems quieter than others? Could it be carpets, curtains, textured walls, and so on? Challenge them to think about how they could find out which materials are better than others at muffling sound. At this stage, focus on what to consider for planning a comparative test. Use two materials per group and a planning board framework. Focus on key features such as:

❖ What will they systematically change? (Type of material, e.g. fabric, and newspaper.)
❖ What will they measure? (Sound level when object is wrapped up in material.)
❖ What will they keep the same? (The number of layers of each material, the object that makes the sound, the volume of the sound from a clock, radio or tape recorder, the position/distance of the sound meter or computer sensor.)
❖ What will the recording table will look like?

Type of material	Sound (measurement unit)
Newspaper	

Group or individual activities

The children plan their investigation and the teacher checks it. They predict which will be best and carry out the investigation, recording findings in a table.

Plenary session
Co-ordinate the review of the results. Different groups have obtained different results from different materials, so it is important to collate the results for each material either on the board or on a computer spreadsheet, such as Claris Works or Excel. Two children could input the data and be taught how the spreadsheet can calculate averages. The spreadsheet could be used to produce a bar graph which should aid interpretation of the evidence related to this investigation.

Points for assessment

❖ Can the children plan the investigation?
❖ Can they measure the sound either with a meter or sensor?
❖ Do they understand that averages are more reliable than single readings?
❖ Do they know that their results for this investigation should be drawn as a bar graph? Can they interpret a bar graph to answer their investigative question?
❖ Do they know that some materials are better than others at muffling sound?

Teacher's own notes:

Understanding primary science

Chapter 5
Materials

Everything is made of one or more materials. Children tend to associate the word 'material' with fabrics or building materials, but scientifically the term includes every **solid**, **liquid** and **gas** that is known. Many materials occur naturally, e.g. stone, rock, soil, wood, air, water, etc, whereas others have been made by human beings. Many foods such as bread are made from natural products. Humans make fabrics, medicines, plastics, metals, fertilisers, herbicides, rubber, pottery, glass and many other everyday products.

What are materials made of?

All materials are made of very tiny particles called **atoms**. Atoms in turn are composed of even smaller sub particles.

The diagram below (**Figure 41**) shows a hydrogen atom. Pure hydrogen is an example of an element. It has only one **proton**, **neutron** and **electron**.

Figure 41

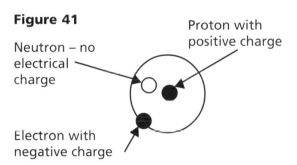

Neutron – no electrical charge

Proton with positive charge

Electron with negative charge

Atoms can join with other atoms to form larger particles called **molecules**, e.g. two oxygen atoms form an oxygen molecule and because it is made from only one type of atom it is also classified as being an **element**. A molecule of water is made of two hydrogen atoms and one oxygen atom. Water is an example of a **compound**

Atomic particle	Location and properties
Proton	Centre or **nucleus** of atom and carries a positive electrical charge
Neutron	Centre or **nucleus** of atom; equal in number to the protons; carries no electrical charge
Electrons	In **orbit** around the nucleus; carries a negative electrical charge

because it is made of more than one type of atom. Any substance that is made up of two or more different atoms is a compound. There are hundreds of different chemical compounds that make up all biological and other materials.

All elements are characterised by the number of electrons they have in each atom. The number of electrons is balanced by the number of protons. The electrons are located in a series of concentric shells. The shell next to the nucleus can only hold two electrons but the next three shells can hold eight, eight and 18 electrons. For example, a carbon atom has six electrons and six protons; an oxygen atom has eight electrons around each nucleus and eight protons in the nucleus (**Figure 42**).

Figure 42

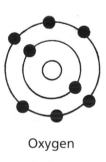

Oxygen

There are more than a hundred different elements and each has a precise number of electrons. Elements can combine with other elements and this is what gives such a vast range of different materials. A material made by combining one or more different types of atom makes a compound. Water is one of the most important compounds on Earth. A particle or molecule of water consists of two atoms of hydrogen joined with one atom of oxygen (**Figure 43**).

Figure 43

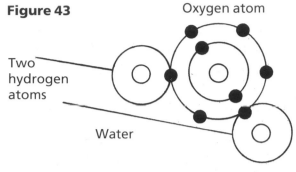

Two hydrogen atoms

Oxygen atom

Water

Bonding

Atoms can be held together in different ways.

There are three ways in which atoms can be held together. They are all types of **chemical bonding** and include:

▲ covalent bonding;
▲ ionic bonding;
▲ metallic bonding.

Covalent bonding

A water particle (molecule) is an example of covalent bonding. Covalent bonds occur when electrons are shared between atoms. The electrons in the outer shell of two hydrogen atoms are shared with the six electrons in the second shell of an oxygen atom giving a stable number of eight electrons in the second shell.

Ionic bonding

A good example of ionic bonding is common salt – chemical name **sodium chloride**. Sodium chloride consists of a metallic element – sodium and a non-metallic element – chlorine. Sodium atoms have 11 electrons arranged in three outer shells: two, eight and one. Chlorine atoms have 17 electrons in the first three orbital shells as two, eight and seven. The 'sharing' of the single electron from the outer shell of a sodium atom to the outer shell of a chlorine atom bonds the two atoms together by creating ionic forces (**Figure 44**).

Figure 44

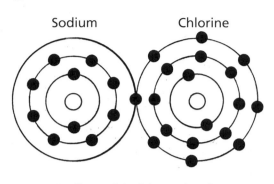

Sodium   Chlorine

Sodium chloride molecule

An **ion** is an atom that has lost or gained an electron. In the electron transfer the chorine atom gains a full complement of eight electrons in the outer shell. Thus the sodium atom becomes a sodium ion and has a positive charge because it has lost an electron. The chlorine atom becomes a negative chlorine ion because it gains a negative electron from sodium. Strong electrostatic forces bind the atoms together to create a cubic crystal structure.

Metallic bonding

Metals lose electrons and form positive ions. Metals are held together in lattice structures surrounded by the lost electrons. Electrostatic forces attract the electrons and metallic ions to each other. This creates very stable materials that are strong, malleable and hard.

Properties of materials

There are many types of materials and these are grouped according to their properties. There are several criteria that can be used to classify or sort materials and include:

- ▲ colour;
- ▲ transparent, opaque or translucent;
- ▲ magnetic or non-magnetic;
- ▲ conductor or insulator of electricity;
- ▲ hard or soft;
- ▲ how much it stretches – elasticity;
- ▲ hardness;
- ▲ toughness;
- ▲ flexibility;
- ▲ density – how much matter there is in a unit volume;
- ▲ state of matter: solid, liquid or gas;
- ▲ solubility.

Physically changing materials by using force

If a material is **bent** and does not return to its original position, it is exhibiting **plasticity** and **malleability**. If a wooden ruler is bent it will either return to its original position when the force is removed therefore exhibiting elasticity, or if too much force is applied it will break because the limits of its elasticity have been exceeded.

If a material is **squashed** and retains its new shape it is **malleable** and has exceeded its elastic limits; if an inflated ball is squashed and the force removed it will return to its original shape because of the property of stiffness and elasticity.

Twisting involves applying a turning force to a material. This can be done with dough, paper, elastic, etc. If it does not return to its original shape it exhibits **toughness**. If it breaks it has exceeded its **elastic limit**, and if it returns to its original shape it exhibits toughness. **Stretching** can also be explored with dough, metal springs, wool, rubber bands, elastic, etc. If the material is stretched it may retain the stretching illustrating it is **ductile**; if it breaks it has exceeded the elastic limit of the material and if it returns to the original shape it illustrates **stiffness**.

Density

The **density** of a material will determine if it **floats or sinks**. Density depends on how tightly particles are packed in a given space or volume. The amount of material in a piece of substance is known as that substance's **mass**.

Mass, unlike **weight**, does not change. For example if a kilogram of lead was transported to the Moon it would still have the same amount of matter or 'stuff' in it, and so its mass would be unchanged. On Earth it would weigh 1.0 Newton, i.e. have a pull force due to gravity of 1.0 Newton. However, its weight would be different because weight is due to the pull down force of

gravity on the material. The Earth is six times more massive than the Moon. The Moon exerts a pull force that is one sixth as big as that on Earth. Therefore the lead would weigh only 0.16 Newtons on the Moon even though it has the same amount of matter on both the Moon and the Earth. A Newton is a standard international (SI) unit for force.

The density of an object is the amount of material in a unit volume. For example, 100 grams of liquid water has a volume of 100cm^3. Therefore, every gram occupies one cubic centimetre.

Materials that have more than one gram of matter in a cubic centimetre of the material will be more dense than water and so will not float in water but sink. Materials that have less matter than one gram of matter in a cubic centimetre will be less dense than water and so will float. See also lesson plans and subject knowledge notes on 'forces'.

Water expands when it freezes so there is more space for every gram of the particles. This makes the density of ice less than one gram per cubic centimetre, and so it floats on the liquid water.

Figure 45

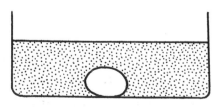

Ball of plasticine sinks. More dense than water.

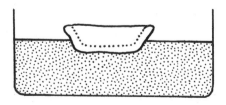

Boat shape plasticine now takes up more space and floats: now less dense than water.

It is possible to change the shape of materials that sink. For example a ball of Plasticine sinks. If its shape is changed into a boat shape, then air is introduced into the 'hull' of the material. The material now has a larger volume because it has had air introduced into it. There is now less than one gram of material – air plus Plasticine – for every cubic centimetre of volume the shape occupies – so its density has fallen. When the density of the Plasticine boat shape becomes less than one gram per cubic centimetre the shape will float on water (**Figure 45**).

Properties of solids, liquids and gases

A **solid** has a fixed shape and volume, cannot be poured but can be cut. Particles (atoms and molecules) from which the solid is made are held close together by bonds or strong forces between the atom and cannot move about freely. In a **liquid** the particles are able to move about freely so the liquid takes the shape of the container it is in. Liquids can be poured because they flow well. A **gas** has particles widely spaced so that they have no fixed shape or volume. It is possible to compress a gas and change it into a liquid, e.g. liquid oxygen is stored in metal cylinders and used in hospitals.

Magnetic materials

Magnetic materials are made of special materials that include iron, cobalt and nickel, and alloys made of mixtures including one or more of these. Magnetic materials are attracted or pulled towards metals also containing magnetic materials. Therefore, a magnet will attract any metal material that is magnetic. It will not attract metals that do not have iron, cobalt or nickel in them. Some of the strongest magnets are made from alloys of different metals, e.g. **alnico** magnets are made from aluminium (non-magnetic) and nickel and cobalt that are magnetic. Alnico magnets are strong and exhibit a pulling force over a greater distance than a steel magnet of similar size. All schools should have at least one alnico magnet.

Magnets have two **poles**, one at each end, where most of their pulling and pushing forces are located. If a bar magnet is suspended it will orientate in a north/south direction. The pole pointing north is a 'north-seeking pole' and is attracted to the Earth's magnetic north pole. The opposite end points south and is a 'south-seeking pole'. Unlike poles of a magnet **attract**, and like poles **repel**. Thus the north pole of the magnet attracts a south pole but repels a north pole (**Figure 46**).

Figure 46

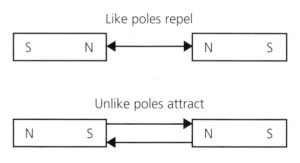

Like poles repel

Unlike poles attract

Conductors and insulators

These terms are used to explain what happens when an electrical current is applied to a material. Those materials that allow an electrical current to flow through are **conductors** and those that do not allow it to flow through are insulators. Conductors include metals and graphite and some chemical solutions. Metals have electrons that are not held strongly and easily move away from the nuclei, whereas insulators have electrons that are firmly held by forces of attraction in their atomic nuclei. When electricity flows through a conductor it warms up because of collisions between the atomic particles in the metal. It is a bit like friction.

When an electric current flows through a conductor it creates a magnetic effect. This can be demonstrated using a coil of wire around a rod of soft iron such as a nail that has had the point made blunt.

Figure 47

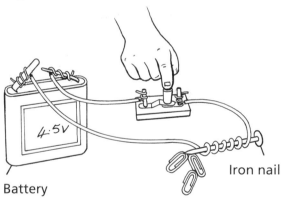

Battery

Iron nail

The electromagnet will pick up paper clips or pins as long as the current flows through the coil of wire (**Figure 47**). The number of coils in the wire and battery voltage affects the strength of the magnetic field.

Insulators of heat energy

Some materials are also good insulators of heat energy. They are good thermal insulators because they prevent heat from moving. Heat energy always moves from a hotter place to a cooler place. There has to be a difference in temperature for heat to be transferred. Thermal insulators slow down the rate at which heat is transferred, e.g. wool, polyester fleece, plastic foam are good insulators of heat.

Double glazing has air trapped between two layers of glass. The air is a good insulator and reduces heat loss. Picnic cool boxes are insulated to stop heat from the air reaching the food and drink. An igloo stops heat reaching the colder external environment.

We use a thermometer to measure how hot things are and the unit for temperature is 'degrees Celsius' written °C. Other temperature scales should not be taught in science. Children should use alcohol (spirit) thermometers. Avoid using mercury thermometers because mercury is toxic. Data loggers and a computer can also be used to record temperature changes remotely and automatically.

The amount of heat energy stored in an object is the thermal energy and is now measured in **joules**. Older people may have been taught that energy is measured in calories or British Thermal units (BThU), but these have now been replaced by the joule.

Solubility

Some materials, e.g. sugar, can dissolve in liquid such as water. Such substances are **soluble** in water. The water is the **solvent** and the substance that dissolves is the **solute**. The result is a **solution**. For example, sugar can dissolve in water to make a sugar solution (**Figure 48**).

Figure 48

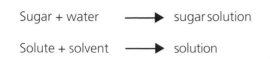

Sugar + water   ⟶   sugar solution

Solute + solvent   ⟶   solution

The sugar may not be visible to the eye when it has **dissolved** and it can be tasted to prove that it has not disappeared. If a sugar solution is evaporated, the water is removed and the solid sugar reappears. **Evaporation** is a process where solvent particles, in this case water, change from liquid form to a gaseous form, and escape from the solution into the air. If sugar is added to the water until no more can dissolve and the sugar is visible on the bottom of the container, then the solution is a **saturated** solution.

In a solution the particles of solute are thoroughly mixed with the solvent. When there is no more space for the solute to mix between the liquid particles then the solute cannot dissolve unless more room is made between the water particles. This can be achieved by warming the solvent, making the solvent particles move apart, and there is hence more space for the solute. More solute can usually be dissolved in the same solvent at higher temperatures than at lower temperatures for the same volume of solvent. Thus, more sugar dissolves in hot water than cold water. However, this is not true for all substances. Common salt, sodium chloride, is an exception. A point is always reached when there is no more room for the solute to mix thoroughly and the solution is then saturated.

Lesson focus: *Materials*

Early Learning Goal: *Knowledge and understanding of the world*

KS1 NC Ref: *Sc1 1, 2b, e–h; Sc3 1a–c*   **Year group:** *Reception*

Scheme of work unit: *1C – Sorting and using materials*

Intended learning: for children to know four kinds of material (wood, plastic, metal and fabric) and to use their senses to sort these into groups.

Resources

❖ A bag of objects made from different materials for the introduction.
❖ Another range of different everyday objects made from wood, plastic, fabric and metal (avoid objects with sharp points).
❖ Sorting trays/boxes with heads and smiley faces labelled 'William Wood', 'Peter Plastic', 'Molly Metal' and 'Freda Fabric'.

Introduction: *Whole class session*

The teacher introduces the bag containing different objects. Invite children in turn to feel in the bag, describe what the object feels like and guess what it is. The object is then removed from the bag and shown to the class. The teacher asks what the object is made from and talks about the material. S/he checks that the children know that 'material' means more than our everyday use, as in 'curtain material'. Then introduce sorting boxes/trays. These have names to help children associate the object with the name of the material from which it is made. Explain the task: they have to observe the objects and allocate them to the right 'material person'.

Group or individual activities

Children sort the range of objects into categories. The teacher checks their understanding and, if necessary, challenges them to find some more objects in the room and add them to the correct tray.

Plenary session

Groups of children take it in turns to share a collection of sorted objects from a tray. The teacher asks other children in turn what the object is and what it is made from. S/he writes the 'material word' on cards and later adds them to the class language board.

Points for assessment

❖ Do the children know what 'material' means?
❖ Can they recognise metal, wood, plastic and fabric?

Teacher's own notes:

Lesson focus: *Materials*

KS1 NC Ref: *Sc1 2b, c, e–j; Sc3 1c*   **Year group:** *Y1/2*

Scheme of work unit: *1C – Sorting and using materials*

Intended learning: for children to know that some metal materials are magnetic but most things are not.

Resources
- Magnets (for example wand, bar or horseshoe magnets).
- Variety of metal objects made from iron/steel, aluminium, nickel, copper, or simple paper clips, etc, with no sharp edges.
- A range of non metals (for example, woods, plastics, fabrics, etc).
- Sorting trays.
- Prepared pictogram outline.

Introduction: *Whole class session*

Discuss what a metal is and how metals are different from other materials. Introduce a wand magnet if possible – children may be unfamiliar with this sort of magnet as it is covered in plastic. Ask the children if they know what it is and what it does. Invite a child to hold it and test it near a heap of paper clips. They may be surprised by the moving paper clips. The challenge is for the children to choose a range of objects, either in the collection or in the room, draw and write the name of the object in a table, predict if it is magnetic and record the magnet test using a table format provided by the teacher.

Material (metal or not metal)	**My prediction** *Magnetic* *Non-magnetic*	

Group or individual activities

Children carry out their tests in small groups, recording individual predictions and results. They draw a picture of one of their group testing a material with a magnet.

Plenary session

The children share their results and the teacher co-ordinates these using a table on the board. The teacher uses questions such as:

- Which things were magnetic?
- What were they made of?
- Which things were not attracted to the magnet?
- What were they made of?

S/he helps them make the connection that only some metals (iron, steel, nickel) are magnetic, and that other metals (aluminium, copper, gold, etc) are not magnetic. The children then draw pictures to add to a pictogram which the teacher has started on a chart. The teacher checks with them as they stick them on the pictogram. S/he then uses it to tell the story of their magnet survey.

Points for assessment

❖ Do the children know some materials are magnetic and some are not magnetic?
❖ Do they know that only some metals are magnetic?
❖ Can they record in a table outline?
❖ Can they contribute to a pictogram?
❖ Do they know what the pictogram represents?

Teacher's own notes:

Lesson focus: *Materials*

KS2 NC Ref: *Sc1 2a, b, e, f, h–m; Sc3 1a*   **Year group:** *Y3/4*

Scheme of work unit: *3C – Characteristics of materials*

Intended learning: for children to be able to plan and carry out a fair test on how well materials wear.

Resources
- Three different types of fabric (for example denim, wool or cotton).
- Wood block covered with coarse sand paper.
- Plastic spoons.
- Digital kitchen scales.

Introduction: *Whole class session*

Review children's knowledge of materials and how we use them. Then introduce the three fabrics: denim, wool and cotton. Discuss how the children could find out which is the hardest-wearing material (wood block covered with coarse sand paper can be used to rub the material to wear it). Support them in planning a fair test. They will need to change the type of fabric, measure or judge the number of rubs to make a hole or rub for a certain number of times and collect the 'worn away' fabric. This could be judged qualitatively (for example, not much, quite a lot, a lot) or measured (for example, number of plastic spoonfuls of worn away fabric, mass of fabric worn away). They will need to use the same block, the same size of fabric and try and rub each fabric equally hard to make the test fair. The teacher should provide a table outline for the children to record their results.

Type of fabric	Number of rubs/amount of worn away fabric collected (to match what the children decide to measure)
Denim	

Group or individual activities

The children carry out their rub test. They choose how to judge the wear, and test and measure this, recording in their table outline. The teacher checks how they measure, intervening if errors are spotted and to check that they can explain that their test is fair.

Plenary session

The teacher co-ordinates the sharing of group results. By collecting each group's results, s/he can teach that for those groups who measured the same thing (for example number of rubs to make a hole), the class has obtained repeat readings for that test. The importance of repeat readings is discussed and the teacher stresses that the results can only be compared if the test was fair. S/he challenges the class to put the fabrics in rank order of wearability. Children are asked to design a leaflet for a parent advising them which fabric to choose for a child who enjoys hard physical play. The leaflets will form part of a class display.

Points for assessment

❖ Can the children plan a fair test with support?
❖ Can they measure appropriately and record results in a table?
❖ Can they use the table to draw conclusions and apply their findings to a useful everyday context?
❖ Do they know that materials have different properties?

Teacher's own notes:

Lesson focus: *Materials*

KS2 NC Ref: *Sc1 2a, b, d–m; Sc3 2a*   **Year group:** *Y5/6*

Scheme of work unit: *3C – Characteristics of materials*

Intended learning: for children to know that there is a limit to the mass of a solid (sugar) that can dissolve in a given volume of water; to be able to carry out a fair test, repeat readings and use evidence.

Resources

❖ Sugar, measuring cylinders, digital kitchen scales, spoons, transparent plastic beakers.

Introduction: *Whole class session*

Ask children how they could find out if there is a limit to the amount of sugar that will dissolve in water. Explore their ideas focusing on:

❖ how they would know when no more sugar dissolves;
❖ how volume, temperature and stirring the water could affect the amount of sugar that dissolves;
❖ how to measure how much sugar dissolves.

From this range of ideas, it should be possible to plan a test to which all groups can later pool findings (for example if they decide to vary the volume of water each time: Group A could find out how much sugar dissolves in 10cm³, B in 20cm³, C in 30cm³). Revise the advantage and importance of repeat readings and obtain a class decision for recording results.

Group or individual activities

Children carry out their allocated test. They weigh a beaker with the relevant amount of water and add teaspoons of sugar until no more dissolves, even when it has been stirred. They re-weigh the beaker and by subtraction find the amount of sugar that dissolved. The teacher checks some groups' measurements and calculations for accuracy. Children repeat this three times for their allocated volume and find an average. They record their group's average result on to a class table prepared by the teacher on the board.

Volume of water cm³	Average mass of sugar dissolved (g)
10	
20	
30	
40	
50	

Plenary session

The teacher helps children focus on the salient features of their results by asking one group to explain what they did. This helps the children to know that the results are only usable if every group follows the same procedure. It makes the evidence believable. From the results the children make the connection that as the volume of water increases, the amount of sugar that dissolves increases. But whatever the volume there is still a limit to the amount that will dissolve. S/he then discusses with the children why there is such a limit, and explores their ideas. They communicate their understanding in pairs using writing and drawings to explain the changes that happen as the sugar is added to water until no more dissolves. Usable analogies or models arising from this writing are shared later with the whole class.

Points for assessment

❖ Can the children measure and find an average of repeat readings?
❖ Can they decide if their test was fair and justify this?
❖ Can they see patterns in their results?
❖ Do they know that there is a limit to the mass of sugar that can dissolve in a certain volume of water?

Teacher's own notes:

Chapter 6
Change

Knowledge for materials and change is closely related. Information in the chapter on materials will reinforce useful knowledge needed to teach change effectively, especially your personal knowledge of atomic particles and dissolving.

There are two main types of change: **physical** change and **chemical** change.

Physical change

A physical change is characterised by changes in which **no new substance** is created. Every substance has its own unique characteristic, e.g. water is a substance and has a definite boiling and freezing point of $100°C$ and $0°C$ respectively. When water changes state as a result of heating or cooling, these changes are manifestations of physical changes. If ice is heated to its **melting point**, it changes to liquid water. If liquid water is heated to its **boiling point** it changes to a gas. If **gaseous water** is cooled it **condenses** to **liquid water** and if liquid water is cooled to its **freezing point** it becomes a **solid**. These are all physical changes because the substance is still water, albeit in a different state. Melting point temperatures and freezing point

temperatures are the same. Boiling point and condensing point temperatures are the same. Physical changes are **reversible** – you can get back to the same substance you started with (**Figure 49**).

Figure 49

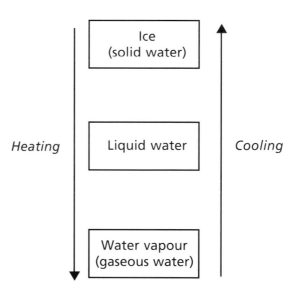

All substances have their own unique melting and boiling point temperatures. Melting points and boiling points are characteristics used by scientists to identify materials. Pure substances such as water and candle wax melt at definite temperatures. Additional energy is needed for water to change from ice to water or solid to liquid, but its temperature does not change. Boiling water in a kettle causes the liquid to change to water vapour (gas) but additional energy is needed to bring about the change.

If steam is condensed on the skin it can cause severe scalding. This is because this extra 'stored heat' or latent heat needed to change the state from liquid to gas is released on to the skin as it reverts from gas to liquid. Steam burns are worse than boiling water burns. Change of state is brought about by transferring energy.

When chocolate is melted it melts over a range of temperatures because it is made of more than one substance. 'Cake covering chocolate' and 'eating' chocolate are different because they contain different substances. It is useful with KS1 pupils to make chocolate Rice Krispie buns, using both kinds of chocolate, for children to make comparisons between the types of chocolate on the buns. Melting and solidifying chocolate is another example of a reversible reaction and so illustrates physical change.

Chemical change

If a change is a chemical change it is **irreversible**. New substances are made that are different to those with which you started. For example, when toast is made, the darkened surface is due to slight burning of bread. The bread cannot be converted back to what it was before toasting so it is a chemical change. An indigestion tablet, when added to water, reacts with it to make a fizzy gas – carbon dioxide – that was not present before. A new

substance has been formed so it is a chemical change. Other examples of chemical change include rusting of metals, making yoghurt, bread and wine, burning candles, coal, petrol, gas, wood and sugar. In all cases the bonds joining atoms together are broken and new ones are formed as atoms are rearranged to make new substances. (See also the chapter on materials.)

Physical and chemical changes are illustrated during the process of lighting a candle. Some of the candle wax first **melts**, then the liquid travels up the wick where it changes to a gas. These changes are all physical changes. When the 'candle wax gas' burns using oxygen from the air to make carbon dioxide and water, the water and carbon dioxide are new substances so it is a chemical change which is irreversible (**Figure 50**).

Figure 50

Wax melts, then vapourises and then burns

Candle wax is only made of carbon and hydrogen atoms that are bonded together. When it burns, and therefore reacts with oxygen atoms, the bonds holding the atoms together in both the wax and oxygen are broken and re-arranged to form carbon dioxide and water with different compounds (**Figure 51**).

When playdough or bread dough is made, these are examples of chemical

Figure 51

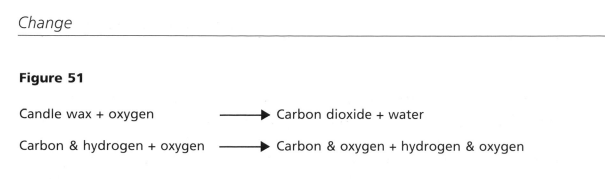

Candle wax + oxygen ⟶ Carbon dioxide + water

Carbon & hydrogen + oxygen ⟶ Carbon & oxygen + hydrogen & oxygen

changes because you cannot get the same ingredients back that you started with. However, if the dough is used for children to change the shape of these materials by bending, squashing, twisting and stretching, they will be causing physical changes because the shapes and changes can be reversed. In fact children will be using forces to bring about the change. The atoms are not broken down, no new bonds are formed – it is still the same modelling substance so it is a physical change.

Mass is conserved

In any type of change whether it is a physical or chemical change, the actual number of particles or atoms remains the same. In other words matter is not created. This is based on the law of conservation of matter which states that matter cannot be created or destroyed only transformed. So, in a chemical reaction where reactions occur between particles to make different substances, the actual number and types of atoms in the system are the same.

In a physical change of, for example, 100g water to ice, there are still 100g of water particles in the ice. The particles are just held differently. In ice (and all solids) the particles are held close together and cannot move freely apart causing solids to have a definite shape. Adding energy to ice will change it to water. In water (and all liquids) the bonds between the particles are less

strongly attracted than in solids and the particles can move freely around each other. Liquids take up the shape of the container they are in because the particles can move freely round each other.

To change state from solid to liquid, energy (heat) has to be added to the material to make the bonds between the particles vibrate and move. If enough energy is added to the system the particles of the material will vibrate sufficiently to be able to move freely apart and the material changes to a gas (**Figure 52**).

Figure 52

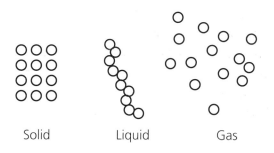

Solid   Liquid   Gas

Gas particles have no definite shape. If these changes are brought about in a closed system the number of water particles will be the same for the ice, water and water vapour. Mass is conserved. In a chemical change, the same atoms present before the reaction are still there. They have just been re-arranged in a different way to make new substances. The mass of atoms is the same before and after the chemical change. Mass is therefore conserved.

Lesson focus: *Change*

Early Learning Goal: *Knowledge and understanding of the world*

KS1 NC Ref: *Sc3 2a*   **Year group:** *Reception*

Scheme of work unit: *2D – Grouping and changing materials*

Intended learning: for children to know that when some things are mixed together they change and can be altered by squashing, bending, twisting and stretching.

Resources
❖ Flour, yeast, salt, vegetable oil, water, mixing bowl, baking tray, spoons, moulds, aprons, oven gloves, access to an oven, flash cards for bend; twist; stretch; squash; large picture of bread display.

Introduction: *Whole class session*

Prior to this lesson the role play/home corner is developing as a café or food shop. Introduce a challenge – the shop or café needs bread to sell. Ask children for ideas about what they need to make bread. As they name a material, place the real material on a table. Any that are missing from their ideas discuss further and show them. Ask the children how the ingredients could be changed into dough.

Group or individual activities

A group of children wash their hands then work with the teacher (or other adult). They mix the dried flour and yeast. They feel it and describe it. They add water and take it in turns to mix it with their hands. The teacher asks them how it has changed and ensures the dough becomes the right consistency. Then each child is given a ball of dough to 'work'.

Challenge them to change the shape of dough by stretching, bending, twisting, squashing. What shapes can they make? The teacher intervenes if the children have misconceptions of the terms bend, squash, twist, stretch, and clarifies the terms through demonstrating the relevant actions. S/he challenges the children in turn to respond to these words to produce new shapes. The children make a shape of their choice and explain how they made it using the key words.

The dough is left to rise in a warm place. The children observe and discuss this change before the bread is cooked. The teacher encourages the children to predict how the bread will change.

Plenary session

The children show the class their bread shapes and explain how they made them. The teacher uses flash cards for stretch, bend, twist, and squash to reinforce the concept. S/he shows a picture of different breads and they discuss how dough would be changed, e.g. French stick would use the stretch card. The picture is later placed where the children can practise placing the flash card words on pictures of different breads, showing 'changing' action.

Points for assessment
❖ Could the children talk about the changes that occur when the ingredients are mixed together?
❖ Can they use the words squash, bend, twist, stretch accurately?

Lesson focus: *Change*

KS1NC Ref: *Sc1 1, 2a–j; Sc3 2b*   **Year group:** *Y1/2*

Scheme of work unit: *2D – Grouping and changing materials*

Intended learning: for children to plan and carry out a test on ice melting and to know that ice melts faster in a warmer place.

Resources
❖ Frozen ice pops and ice cubes of different sizes.
❖ Stop clock.
❖ *Star Science Planning House* framework (Ginn). This contains information on fair tests.

Introduction: *Whole class session*

The teacher draws a plan of the classroom on the board. S/he explains that s/he has some ice and that s/he needs to know where best to keep it from melting if the freezer breaks down. They discuss which would be the best place in the room to slow down the melting. The teacher helps them to plan a fair test and shows them some ready-made ice cubes of different sizes and some frozen ice pops. They discuss which form of ice (cubes or pops) to use to make their test fair. They decide to use ice pops because at the factory the same amount of liquid is used in each packet whereas the teacher's ice cubes are different sizes.

Group or individual activities

Children place an ice pop in four different places in the room. The ice pop is observed every 15 minutes by touching. As each ice pop begins to melt, the children tell the teacher, who then records the 'melting place' on a large table to support comparisons of the children's findings in the plenary session.

Plenary session

The teacher refers to the table of results. S/he challenges the children to put them in rank order of 'winner' to 'loser' – the one that melted first being the loser. The teacher asks the children if the test was really fair, before challenging them to explain which is the best place in the room to slow down the melting process. Then they draw and write about their test and findings.

Points for assessment
❖ Do they know what a fair test is?
❖ Can they draw conclusions from their results?
❖ Do they know that ice melts quickly in warm places?

Lesson focus: *Change*

KS2 NC Ref: *Sc1 1a, b; 2a–j, l; Sc3 2b*   **Year group:** *Y3/4*

Scheme of work unit: *4C – Keeping warm*

Intended learning: to be able to use and read a thermometer safely and accurately; to know that the temperature of water which is warmer than the room will fall to room temperature, and water which is colder than the room will rise to room temperature.

Resources

❖ Spirit thermometers, range of four 500ml pop bottles containing water at different temperatures (icy cold to very warm).

Introduction: *Whole class session*

Using four plastic bottles containing very warm (not boiling), warm, cold and icy cold water, ask how the bottles could be ordered from hottest to coldest without using measuring instruments. Challenge a child to order them by touch. Discuss the limitations of this method. Ask how it could be made more accurate. Now introduce a spirit thermometer. Teach the children how to remove it from its plastic case and explain why the end stop should not be removed (it stops the thermometer rolling off the table and breaking). Teach them how to hold it by the stem, not the bulb, how to read the scale and that degrees Celsius is the correct unit. Use drawings on the board to teach them how to read the scale. Vary the drawing to show a different temperature until children are reading the scale accurately. When children have this skill, introduce the group task of measuring and recording the temperature of each of the four samples of both water and room, at the beginning and after 15 minutes.

Group or individual activities

Children use thermometers to find the temperature of different samples of water and the room, recording temperatures in a table provided by the teacher. They discuss how the temperatures changed. The teacher interacts with some children who have to tell him or her the temperature. S/he intervenes if necessary to reinforce how to read a thermometer in degrees Celsius.

Plenary session

The children share their findings. The teacher asks them:

❖ What happens to the temperature of the very warm and warm water? (The temperature falls.)
❖ What happens to the temperature of the cold and very cold water? (The temperature rises.)
❖ When do you think the temperature of the warm water will stop falling? How could you find out? (Leave it for longer and record the temperature when the spirit stops moving.)

The teacher explains that the temperature of the warm and cold water will change. Cold and warm water temperatures will change until they are both at room temperature.

Points for assessment

❖ Can children use a thermometer safely and read it accurately?
❖ Do they know that warm water will cool down to the temperature of the room?
❖ Do they know that cold water will warm up to the temperature of the room?

Lesson focus: *Change*

KS2 NC Ref: *Sc1 1b; 2a–m; Sc3 2d, e*　　　　　**Year group:** *Y5/6*

Scheme of work unit: *5D – Changing state*

Intended learning: for children to turn ideas into a form that can be investigated, to plan and carry out a fair test and communicate findings about factors that affect evaporation.

Resources

- ❖ Plastic containers of different shapes.
- ❖ Measuring cylinders.
- ❖ Kitchen weighing scales (digital).
- ❖ Thermometers.
- ❖ Planning board frameworks, e.g. from *Star Science*.

Introduction: *Whole class session*

Discuss and explain evaporation from a previous lesson. Brainstorm and list on the board children's ideas about what causes water to evaporate (e.g. temperature of place, shape of container, depth of water, draughts/wind). Explain that each group will choose one thing from the list to investigate. Work through an example on the board using a planning board framework focusing on:

- ❖ the question they will investigate;
- ❖ what to change;
- ❖ what to measure to obtain evidence to answer the question;
- ❖ what to keep the same to make the test fair;
- ❖ the headings of the two column results table, e.g. 'What I will change' and 'Volume of water left after 2 days'.

Explain what resources are available and that groups must choose what to use.

Group or individual activities

Children choose an idea and turn it into a form that can be investigated. (Those needing most support proceed with the plan that the teacher and the whole class worked through.) They plan the investigation. The teacher checks the plans and encourages them to record their predictions. All groups decide to keep the volume/mass of water the same in each container. Then they proceed with setting up the investigation. The teacher monitors this, checking children's measurements of either volume or mass of water. (It is possible to record rate of evaporation by either measuring volume or mass.) Measurements will be made by groups after a period of two days. Readings of instruments should be checked and, if necessary, small group teaching carried out to ensure accuracy of readings.

Children begin to write up their investigation using the planning board framework for support.

Plenary session

The teacher reviews the planning and setting up of the investigation. S/he discusses:

- ❖ the range of questions being investigated and lists them on the board;
- ❖ how to measure volume and mass accurately;
- ❖ their format for recording;
- ❖ their predictions.

When children have results, the teacher reviews the results with the class. Questions focus on how predictions relate to the results and in which container or which place water evaporated the most. The teacher helps children to make connections to the evidence the children obtained about how shape, warmth, draughts, depth of water, etc, affect the time to evaporate by use of effective questioning.

Points for assessment

❖ Do the children know evaporation of water is a change of state from liquid water to a gas?
❖ Can they raise questions and turn one into an investigation?
❖ Can they plan a fair test?
❖ Can they measure accurately?
❖ Do they use results to make conclusions based on the evidence?

Teacher's own notes:

Chapter 7
Electricity

What is electricity? This is a likely question from children but difficult to answer in ways that children can understand. However, a personal understanding will help you teach it more confidently and support your decisions about how to address such questions in the classroom.

To understand what electricity is you need to know about the structure of particles or atoms that was addressed in Chapter 5 on materials.

Figure 53

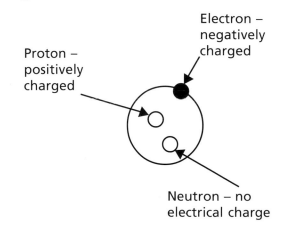

Proton – positively charged

Electron – negatively charged

Neutron – no electrical charge

Remember! Atoms are made up of three types of particles: **protons**, **neutrons** and **electrons** (**Figure 53**). Protons carry positive electrical charges, neutrons are neutral and have no electrical charge, and electrons carry a negative electrical charge. Protons and neutrons are in the centre or nucleus of atoms with negative charged particles of electrons in orbit around the **nucleus**. The positively charged protons in the nucleus attract negatively charged, orbiting electrons and this force stops electrons moving away.

In atoms of some materials such as copper and other conductors that let electricity flow through, an electron is able to move away from its atom. When this happens, an **electric current** is created. Thus when you connect plastic covered copper wire to a torch bulb and battery so that the bulb lights, the battery provides the force to make an electron move from each copper atom. This has a knock-on effect rather like domino toppling, and the vibrating electrons make the bulb light. The electrons move slowly but the result of this knock-on effect is virtually instant. It is the movement of electrons that makes an electric current. So we explain electricity in terms of electrons moving through a metal or other conductor. The electrons are pushed through the copper wire by the force from a battery. Copper and other such materials are **conductors** of electricity.

Insulators

Insulators are the opposite of conductors. They do **not** allow an electric current to pass through them. The plastic material around electrical wire is insulation. Insulators hold all the electrons near the nuclei of their atoms. There are no free electrons that can move in the circuit and an electric current cannot flow through them. Plastic, rubber, wood and glass are all good insulators and prevent the electric current from moving and taking the wrong pathway.

Electrical circuits

For a current to flow there has to be a complete circuit. This provides a continuous link between the battery and components in the circuit. In school, one of the simplest electrical circuits would be a battery, wire, bulb, wire and battery in that order. If there is a gap in the circuit, electric current will not flow.

Switches are devices for opening and closing gaps in the circuit. When the gap is closed the current flows and the switch is in the 'on' position. When the gap is open, the current does not flow because the switch is in the 'off' position. Switches can be easily made using balsa wood as a base material, two brass drawing pins and a paper clip (**Figure 54**).

Unscrewing a torch bulb from a bulb holder will stop the current flow and switch off the circuit. Screwing the bulb into the bulb holder will switch it on (**Figure 55**).

Cells and batteries

What we call a battery is technically a group of **cells**. A 1.5 volt cell is the simplest battery. Three 1.5 volt cells make a battery producing 4.5 volts. Battery is an everyday term and is used here to help the reader, but using science language it is a group of two or more cells.

A battery has a positive and negative terminal. In a 1.5 volt battery the positive terminal is the 'stud' on the top, and the base and the metal case are the negative terminal. Inside a

Figure 54

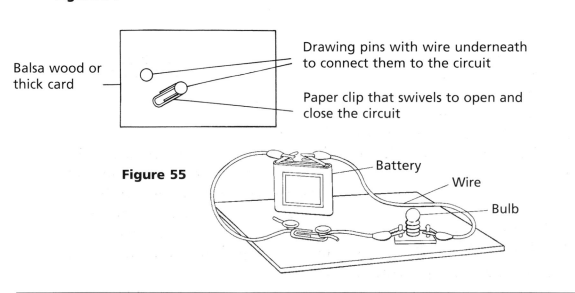

Balsa wood or thick card

Drawing pins with wire underneath to connect them to the circuit

Paper clip that swivels to open and close the circuit

Figure 55

Battery

Wire

Bulb

Figure 56

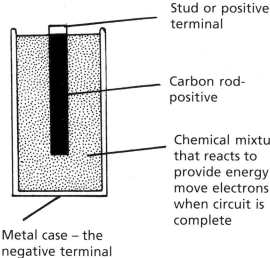

Stud or positive terminal

Carbon rod-positive

Chemical mixture that reacts to provide energy to move electrons when circuit is complete

Metal case – the negative terminal

Figure 57

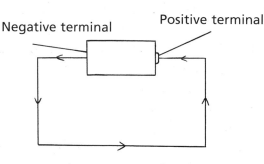

Negative terminal   Positive terminal

Electrons move from negative to positive

battery is a carbon rod that connects to the stud or positive terminal. The carbon rod is 'short of electrons' so is positive. The case of a battery is often made of zinc. Around the carbon rod is a mixture of chemicals that includes manganese dioxide and ammonium chloride (**Figure 56**).

This mixture produces surplus electrons at the negative end of the battery and a shortage of electrons at the positive end. When the circuit is complete electrons get pushed from the negative terminal to the positive one, and electric current flows (**Figure 57**).

A battery is 'flat' when all the chemicals have reacted and it cannot push electrons through the circuit. Young children may find it easier to manipulate 4.5 volt 'flat shaped' batteries that have metal 'knife' terminals.

Measuring electrical force, current and resistance

The force that a battery provides to make electrons move is measured in **volts** using a **voltmeter**. The amount of electricity moving in the circuit is measured in **amperes** or **amps**. An **ammeter** measures electrical current.

Materials that are conductors of electricity will try and stop electricity moving through them. We say they **resist** electricity and each material has a certain **resistance** that can be measured in **ohms** (**Figure 58**). Resistance is calculated using the following formula:

Figure 58

$$\textbf{Resistance} \ = \ \frac{\textbf{voltage}}{\textbf{current}}$$

Current

In theory the amount of current in a circuit is the same at any point. The same current flows through each place. In practice this can be confusing especially if the circuit has two or more bulbs arranged in series one after the other.

Figure 59

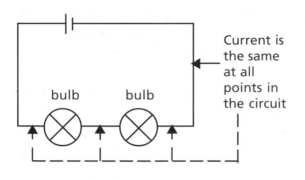

Current is the same at all points in the circuit

If the current is measured at different points in the circuit with an ammeter, it is the same because the current flow is the same. In practice the bulbs may vary in the intensity of light made because their filaments may not be exactly the same and each may offer different levels of resistance. Increasing the length of wire in a circuit increases the resistance. You can show this by using two bulbs each with a different voltage rating. By interchanging the bulbs, the one with the highest resistance still is most bright, so position in the circuit does not affect brightness, but a bulb's resistance does.

How a bulb works

A torch bulb is made of very thin wire that has a big electrical resistance. This means that when the circuit is complete the electrons flow through the copper wire of the connecting wire, through the metal screw thread or stud into the thin wire inside the bulb. Thin wire has a higher resistance than thick wire and it tries to stop the electrons moving (**Figure 60**).

Energy is transferred from the electrons to the wire filament making the particles (atoms) of the filament vibrate

so vigorously that it becomes white hot and emits light. If a switch in the circuit is turned off it stops the battery pushing the electrons in the circuit, so the light goes out.

The filament of a bulb is surrounded by inert gas such as argon that does not react chemically with the metal of the filament. If the filament was surrounded with air containing oxygen it would burn and oxidise into a new substance so ruining the bulb quickly.

Figure 60

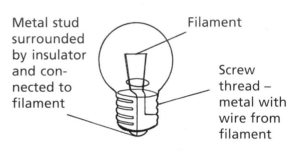

Metal stud surrounded by insulator and connected to filament

Filament

Screw thread – metal with wire from filament

A bulb **blows** when the filament **burns out**. This can happen at the end of the bulb's **life** but it can be speeded up if a battery is used in the circuit that is too powerful for the bulb. Bulbs have voltage ratings printed on the metal screw case. As a general rule the voltage rating for the bulb should be less than that for the battery being used. Thus, if a 4.5 volt battery is being used it is advisable to use a 3.5 volt bulb, i.e. the voltage of the bulb is just less than the voltage rating for the battery.

A 1.5 volt bulb used in a circuit with a 4.5 volt battery is very likely to make the bulb blow because the voltage causes too much flow of energy to the filament which then overheats and melts creating a gap in the bulb and therefore in the circuit. So it is like "switching off". To complete the circuit a new bulb of the correct voltage would need to be used.

Power

Bulbs and other electrical devices use electrical energy. **Power** is measured in **watts** and is a measure of the rate at which electrical energy is transformed into useful energy. **Energy** is measured in **joules**. A watt is the SI unit for measuring power. All electrical devices have a power rating in watts or kilowatts. For example a 100 watt light bulb, when switched on, transforms 100 joules of energy per second into light and heat. In 10 hours of use this light bulb would use 10 ∞ 100 watts = 1,000 watts or 1 kilowatt. Electrical energy is charged in terms of kilowatts of power consumed over a quarter of a year.

Power stations

The electricity used in the home is generated in power stations. Electricity is a form of energy and energy is defined as the ability to do work. Fuels used in some power stations are stores of chemical energy. When burnt they release this energy. The energy released from burning coal is derived from the products of photosynthesis millions of years ago. The light energy used by ancient plants was trapped in fossils and, after mining and transporting to power stations, used to generate heat to make steam. The steam makes turbines move huge coils of wire around magnetic cores. In 1831 Michael Faraday discovered that when a magnet is moved within a coil of wire

it makes electricity. Gas, wood, straw, oil are other examples of fuels that can be used to make steam to generate electricity. The energy from these fuels is transformed as follows:

Chemical energy of the fuel to kinetic energy (movement of turbines) to electrical energy which in turn can be used for lighting, heating, moving, making sound, etc. (**Figure 61**).

Although the energy is conserved in these transformations, some is dissipated to lower grades of energy – heat energy – that is less usable as a resource for human use.

Figure 61

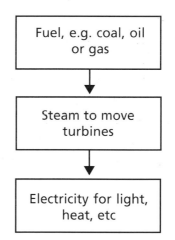

Series and parallel circuits

If components such as bulbs are connected in a line one after the other, they are in **series**. The current at each part of the circuit is the same. But because there are more filaments to flow through than with one bulb, resistance increases and the bulbs glow less brightly than when using a single one. Adding more bulbs is equivalent to adding more wire and so resistance to the current flow increases (**Figure 62**).

Figure 62

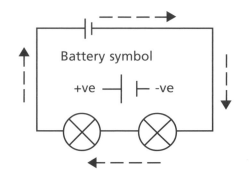

Bulbs wired in **parallel** have a choice of routes for the current to take (**Figure 63**). If the same bulbs are used in a parallel circuit as a series circuit, the bulbs in parallel will glow more brightly because there is less resistance to current flow in each part of the circuit, and the current flow in each part of the circuit is the same. More current can flow in a parallel circuit with two bulbs than in a series circuit with two bulbs. Circuits in parallel shorten the life of a battery faster than in a series circuit with the same components.

Varying the current in a circuit

Current can be varied in a circuit in a number of ways:

- ▲ adding or removing cells (batteries);
- ▲ changing the length of the wire;
- ▲ changing the thickness of the wire;
- ▲ changing the type of wire e.g. copper wire for nichrome wire;
- ▲ changing the voltage rating of bulbs.

If a length of propelling pencil lead – which is really a form of carbon called graphite – is wired into a circuit, the light will dim because the graphite has a high resistance to the flow of electricity. For a long piece of graphite the light will be dim; for a shorter piece of graphite the light will be brighter. If a circuit is made so that the length of graphite varies, a dimmer switch can be made.

Figure 63

Figure 64

Parallel circuit

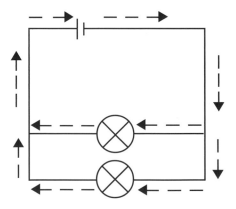

Dimmer switch

4.5 volt battery

bulb

Wire that can slide along graphite to make lamp brighter or dimmer

Graphite

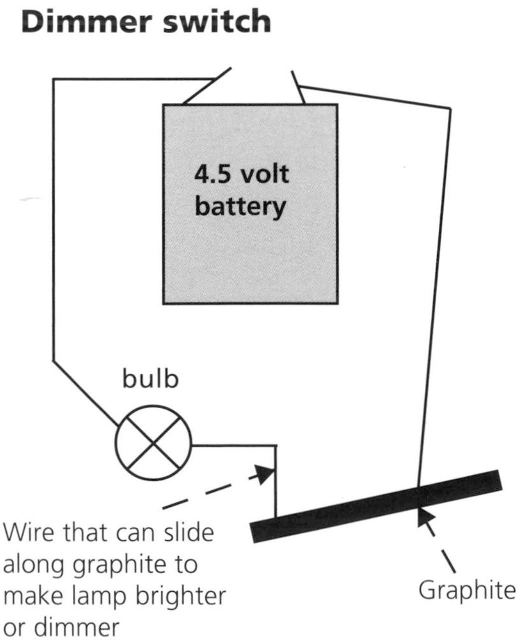

Electrical symbols

Electrical components are represented with standard symbols. These should be used to help children progress from observational drawings to using symbolic representations.

Figure 65

Switch

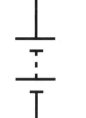

Cell

Battery of Cells

Connecting wire

Junction of wires

Bulb

Motor

Buzzer

Lesson focus: *Electricity*

Early Learning Goal: *Knowledge and understanding of the world*

KS1 NC Ref: *Sc4 1a*   **Year group:** *Reception*

Scheme of work unit: *2F – Using electricity*

Intended learning: for children to know that many everyday things use electricity; some use mains electricity and some use electricity from a battery.

Resources

❖ Paper, glue, old catalogues with pictures of electrical items and battery-operated toys, scissors, some battery-operated items such as a torch or toys, battery.

Introduction: *Whole class session*

Show the children a torch. Ask them how it can be made to work. Discuss their ideas of what makes it work. What do they think is inside the torch which makes it work? Test or demonstrate what happens when the battery is taken out of the torch.

Repeat with another battery-operated item such as a toy. Talk about other objects in the classroom that need mains electricity to make them work, e.g. computer, television and video recorder, lights. Write a list. Discuss safety issues – do not touch mains switches with wet hands or play with mains electricity, etc. Compare safety aspects of 'mains' and 'battery' electricity.

Group or individual activities

Children either draw pictures of items in the classroom which use mains electricity, or select pictures of electrical items from an old catalogue, cut them out and stick them on one side of a large sheet of paper folded in half. On the other side they stick their selected pictures (or pictures they have drawn) of things that work using a battery. The folded paper with two headings 'mains electricity' and 'battery electricity' is an introduction to using a two column table as an organiser.

Plenary session

Children show their posters and explain how they have sorted their items into two categories. The teacher then uses a battery powered item – not shown to the children at the beginning of the lesson – to see if they can:

❖ talk about how it works;
❖ predict what would happen if the battery was removed.

S/he lets some children try this in front of the class to test their prediction. To reinforce this work the teacher leaves pictures of electrical items mounted on card on the interactive table, with two sets of labels 'mains electricity' and 'battery electricity', and challenges children to match the item to the correct label during the rest of the week.

Points for assessment

❖ Ask the children to name some everyday things that use mains electricity. Do they know some things that work from a battery?
❖ Ask them to talk about the dangers of using mains electricity and how to use it safely.

Lesson focus: *Electricity*

KS1 NC Ref: *Sc1 2b, 2e–i; Sc4 1b* **Year group:** *Y1/2*

Scheme of work unit: *2F – Using electricity*

Intended learning: for children to know that an electric bulb will not work if there is a break in the circuit and that some materials can complete the circuit. To communicate their findings in drawings and a two column table.

Resources

❖ 4.5v 'flat shaped' battery, four insulated wires with crocodile clips attached, small piece of wood with two nails about 2cm apart fixed vertically into it.

❖ Each nail has a crocodile clip attached, bulb and bulb holder with crocodile leads clipped to it. These are fixed to the top of the plastic drinks bottle – used to make a model lighthouse.

❖ A collection of materials such as plastic spoon, metal spoon, rulers, pieces of copper, aluminium foil, i.e. metals and non-metals.

Introduction: *Whole class session*

Revise how to make a bulb light using a bulb, battery and two wires. Ask two children to demonstrate this. Introduce a model lighthouse either made by you before the lesson or maybe by an older group of children. Discuss and point out the electrical components – bulb, wires, battery. Ask why it is not working. (Answer: the circuit is not complete because of the gap between the nails.) What would happen if the crocodile clips were taken off the nails and then joined or touched? Try it and see the bulb light. Challenge the children to find other ways of lighting the bulb and lighthouse – while the clips are joined to the nails.

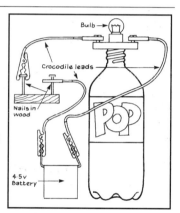

Group or individual activities

The group of children discuss the challenge in small groups and plan what to try. They share their ideas with the teacher before trying them out. The teacher listens and intervenes with questions or further prompts if necessary. The children begin to place objects across the gap between the nails and note which ones make the bulb light and those which do not. They sort them into two sets.

Plenary session

Ask the children to show how they met the challenge and what they found out. Discuss the materials that made the bulb light. Do they notice that metals cause the light to switch on and most non-metals do not? (NB graphite – pencil lead – a non-metal, will cause the bulb to light!) The teacher helps them to make this 'mental connection'. Emphasise that the circuit had to be complete for the bulb to light and so objects had to be placed across the gap and touch **both** nails to complete the circuit. They draw a picture of the lighthouse and those objects that made the bulb light and those that did not light the bulb. Some children used a two column table provided by the teacher to organise their results. The lighthouse is left on a tinkering table for children to 'play' at finding objects that will light the lighthouse.

Points for assessment

❖ Do they know that a complete circuit is needed for a bulb to light?

❖ Do they know that some everyday objects can be used to complete a circuit of a battery and bulb?

❖ Can they draw the lighthouse circuit pictorially and record appropriately using the two column table format?

Lesson focus: *Electricity*

KS2 NC Ref: *Sc1 2b–f, j, l, m; Sc4 1a, b*   **Year group:** *Y3/4*

Scheme of work unit: *4F – Circuits and conductors*

Intended learning: for children to systematically investigate changing bulbs and batteries in a circuit and know that the brightness of the bulb depends on the voltage of the battery and the number of bulbs in the circuit.

Resources

- ❖ Batteries: 1.5 volt and 4.5 volt.
- ❖ Bulbs of different voltage: 1.5 volt and 3.5 volt (voltage is printed on the side of the metal screw of the bulb).
- ❖ Bulb holders, insulated wire, wire strippers, small electrical screwdrivers.
- ❖ Small switch (could be home made from paper clips and drawing pins).

Introduction: *Whole class session*

Revise the components needed for an electrical circuit to work. Discuss the challenges which are:

- ❖ to systematically change the number of bulbs in a circuit and note what happens;
- ❖ to systematically add an extra battery to a circuit and note what happens to the brightness of the bulb.

With teacher guidance some children set up a circuit with one battery, one bulb and a switch as a demonstration and revision for the class. The voltage of the bulb is matched so that it is less than that of the battery, e.g. use a 3.5 volt bulb with a 4.5 volt battery. The teacher comments on the skills needed to make the circuit. S/he then explains the challenges:

- ❖ that each group has to make this circuit and then add an extra bulb;
- ❖ that each group has to add an extra battery.

S/he asks the children to record what they think will happen in each case and give reasons for their predictions.

Group or individual activities

Children discuss their plans in groups. The teacher gives support where necessary. They share their plans with the teacher before they try out their ideas. They record their observations.

Plenary session

The class share their findings. The teacher uses some circuits children have made for each of the challenges and discusses them with the class. S/he reinforces scientific knowledge through effective questioning and explaining, for example, that if extra bulbs are added to a circuit, the bulbs are not as bright as when there is only one bulb; that if an extra battery is added to the circuit the bulb becomes brighter and might 'blow' if the voltage is too high. (The total voltage for a circuit with two batteries is found by adding the voltage of each battery. If it exceeds the voltage of the bulb the bulb is likely to blow.) Children draw and write about their challenges and begin to make generalisations about changing brightness of bulbs in a circuit.

Points for assessment

Can the children add extra bulbs to a circuit? Do they know that adding extra bulbs in a circuit affects their brightness? Do they know that an extra battery in a circuit can make bulb(s) brighter? Do they know that a battery with a high voltage makes a bulb brighter than one with a lower voltage? Do they know that a high voltage bulb with a lower voltage battery makes the bulb dimmer?

Lesson focus: *Electricity*

KS2 NC Ref: *Sc4 1c*   **Year group:** *Y5/6*

Scheme of work unit: *6G – Changing circuits*

Intended learning: for children to know the conventional symbols for electrical components and to use them to make circuits presented to them in symbolic form.

Resources
- ❖ Some batteries.
- ❖ 1.5v battery holders or 4.5v.
- ❖ Bulbs, insulated wire with bared ends, small switches, motors, bell, buzzer, screwdrivers.
- ❖ Worksheet showing pictures of actual components and conventional symbols for components and some circuits for children to construct from symbolic circuit diagrams (see *Star Science Electricity* Upper Junior Pupils' Book).
- ❖ Circuit diagrams from car manual or washing machine manual as overhead projection transparency.
- ❖ Overhead projector.
- ❖ Electrical quiz board (either ready-made or for more able children to make, using: A3 or bigger thick card, brass paper fasteners, pictures of electrical components and their respective symbols, 4.5 volt, knife terminal battery, bulb holder and bulb, four leads with crocodile clips, insulated wire with bared ends, Blu-tack).

Introduction: *Whole class session*
Using a ready-made circuit, revise the components needed for an electrical circuit to work. Draw each component as it appears as an actual observational drawing of the circuit. Discuss how humans have devised accepted ways of communicating using symbols to represent things for example, multiplication in maths is represented by the symbol 'x'. In electrical work scientists and electricians use symbols to represent components. Show an electrical circuit diagram on the overhead projector. Introduce the symbols for bulb, battery or 'cell', wire, switch, motor. Discuss these and draw a circuit diagram by the side of the observational drawing made at the introduction of the lesson. Issue a worksheet with symbols and two different circuit diagrams. The challenge is for the children to interpret the circuit diagrams and make them.

Group or individual activities
Children discuss their circuit diagrams in groups. The teacher gives support where necessary. They make their circuits from the diagrams and test to see if they work. The teacher circulates around the groups checking and intervening where necessary.

Plenary session
The class share their findings and the teacher checks for accurate knowledge of using electrical symbols. To develop understanding and reinforce knowledge of symbols, s/he introduces either as a picture or ready-made, a quiz board.

This has pictures of electrical items stuck on the left-hand side with Blu-tack and by the side of each one is a brass paper fastener. On the right hand side are electrical symbols but they are not matched horizontally. On the back of the board, insulated wire correctly connects 'picture and symbol'. A bulb is fixed to the top of the board and has two long leads, one of which is attached to a 4.5 volt battery, the other is 'free'. The battery also has two leads, one attached to the bulb, the other 'free'. Children are challenged to touch one crocodile clip to the brass fastener by the side of the picture and match this to the correct symbol. If correct, the bulb lights up. Alternatively children in groups could now make their own quiz board or create circuit diagrams and swap them with other groups before making the circuits from symbolic diagrams.

Points for assessment

❖ Do the children know the conventional symbol for each item they used?
❖ Can they create circuits using circuit diagrams provided by the teacher?
❖ Can they draw circuit diagrams which other children can make successfully?

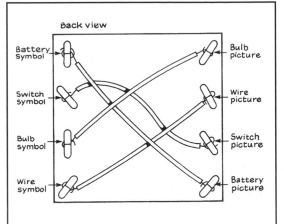

Teacher's own notes:

Chapter 8
Environment

Teaching about the environment requires knowledge of:

- ▲ the variety of life;
- ▲ different environments and their physical factors;
- ▲ habitats and ecosystems;
- ▲ adaptation;
- ▲ principles of feeding.

The variety of living things

Several attempts have been made to classify the wide variety of life. A recent method using five kingdoms for classifying all forms of life is shown below.

Viruses are not included in this classification because they are intermediate between living and non-living things. They only appear to be alive when inside living cells where they can reproduce. Viruses cause diseases such as the common cold, influenza, chickenpox and measles. In some forms of classification micro-organisms are considered to include **bacteria**, **fungi**, viruses and **protista** because they are only visible with a microscope.

Bacteria can be genetically manipulated by scientists to produce medicines, e.g. insulin for diabetics. Some types of bacteria are also used extensively in the yoghurt industry. A useful fungus is yeast which is used in

Kingdom	Features	
Monera	Micro-organisms such as bacteria	
Protista	Single celled animals, e.g. Amoeba	
Fungi	Multicelluar organisms that feed on dead remains and waste products of other living things	
Plants	Multicellular organisms that make their own food by photosynthesis	
Animals	Multicellular and feed on other living things – usually mobile and sensitive to their environment	

Plant group	Features	
Mosses and liverworts	Simple leaves; live in damp places; need water to reproduce	
Ferns	Have roots, stems and leaves that are called fronds; lower side of fronds bear spore producing structures; spores germinate to produce sexual reproductive structures	
Conifers	Large plants with roots, stems and leaves; bear cones for reproducing; usually retain leaves through winter, e.g. Christmas trees	
Flowering plants	Huge variety; all produce flowers that bear reproductive organs; fruits bearing seeds produced as a product of reproduction	

the baking and brewing industries. Plants include four main groups: mosses, ferns, conifers and flowering plants (see table above).

Animals

In the animal kingdom there are two main sub groups: animals without backbones or **invertebrates** and those with backbones or **vertebrates** (see tables opposite).

Species

Within each group of organisms there are different **species**. A species is a group of living things that are able to inter-breed and produce fertile offspring that if successfully reared can reproduce at maturity to maintain the species. For example a horse is a species. It can reproduce to produce fertile young. So can a donkey. But if a horse and donkey are mated they produce a mule. Mules cannot interbreed – they are infertile – so mules are not a species.

Different environments and their physical factors

The term **environment** encompasses all the physical conditions that exist in a place where something lives. There are marine, freshwater, deciduous and coniferous forests, desert, alpine, rainforest, tundra and grassland environments or **biomes**. These large environments or biomes cover all areas of the Earth and within each environment has its own climatic features. Living things are found in all these environments. The place where something lives is the **habitat**. A habitat must provide food, shelter from harsh climatic conditions and predators, and a place to breed. For example a robin's habitat can be a territory within a garden, which provides food and shelter. The environment will also be suitable for nesting and raising young.

An **ecosystem** consists of the organisms and their physical environment. For example, a pond consists of different types of animals and plants within an aquatic environ-

Invertebrates	Features
Coelenterates	Two layers of cells, have tentacles and use sting cells to capture prey, e.g. sea anemones, jelly fish, hydra
Flatworms	Flatworms often found in freshwater, usually black, can replace missing body parts
Segmented worms	Round worms with many repeating body segments; hermaphrodite, e.g. earthworms
Molluscs	Have a smooth body and frequently have a shell, e.g. snails, slugs
Echinoderms	Have a spiny outer case with several arms giving a star shape, all are marine, e.g. starfish
Crustaceans	Have jointed limbs and hard external skeleton; many live in sea, e.g. crabs, lobsters; some live on land, e.g. wood louse; some live in freshwater, e.g. water hog louse, freshwater shrimp
Myriapods	Have many jointed legs, e.g. millipedes and centipedes
Arachnids	These include spiders. They have two main body parts and eight legs
Insects	Have three main body parts: head, thorax and abdomen; there are three pairs of legs; one pair on each thoracic segment; some insects undergo complete metamorphosis during their lifecycle, e.g. butterfly – egg – caterpillar – pupa – butterfly; others emerge from eggs as small replicas of their parents, e.g. grasshopper; this is an example of incomplete metamorphosis

Vertebrates	Features
Fish	Live in water, breathe through gills, have bodies covered in scales; use fins for balance and movement
Amphibians	Undergo complete change of form; eggs laid in water, hatch into free swimming tadpoles; tadpoles change into adults that can live on both land and water, e.g. frog, toad
Reptiles	Have a dry, waterproof skin covered in scales; eggs laid on land, e.g. turtles, snakes
Birds	Have wings; eggs laid in nests and incubated by parents; parental care for young; have a constant body temperature
Mammals	Have a constant body temperature; body has hair; young develop in female body; after birth young feed on mother's milk, e.g. cats, dogs, humans

ment that has varying temperatures, light intensities, dissolved oxygen levels, dissolved nutrients, etc. The collection of all the animal and plants, protista, monera and fungi in the pond form a **community** of living things.

Adaptation

Living things found in ecosystems have adapted in different ways so that they can survive in it. In deciduous woodlands, bluebells are adapted to flower and make seeds before the tree canopy reduces the light reaching the ground. Bluebells have stores of food in bulbs. They are like onions. The store of food enables bluebells to begin growing in late winter so they utilise maximum light for photo-synthesis before the trees gain their leaves. Polar bears are adapted to living in arctic conditions by having thick fur, short noses and small ears to reduce body heat loss. All living things have adapted in various ways to survive in particular environments.

Principles of feeding

A **food chain** is a way in which we represent the flow of energy through an ecosystem. Food chains nearly always begin with plants – **producers** of food. Green plants need sunlight to make food, and the Sun's energy is the ultimate source of energy for nearly all life. The known exceptions are near volcanic vents in the ocean beds and within the crust of the Earth where bacteria utilise sulphur to produce their own food.

Herbivores eat plants and **carni-vores** eat herbivores. Herbivores are also known as primary consumers,

and carnivores are secondary and/or tertiary consumers. Some animals eat both plants and animals and they are **omnivores**.

An animal that is eaten by another animal is the **prey** and the animal that eats it is the **predator**. The process of predators eating prey is **predation**. The following shows a food chain in a pond (**Figure 66**).

Figure 66

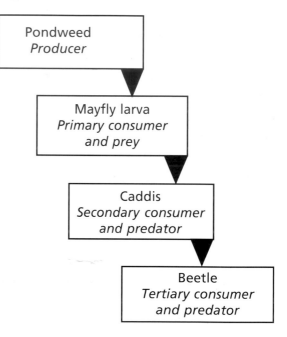

Micro-organisms decompose dead and waste products of living things. This returns the nutrients within dead bodies and waste products to the ecosystem and carbon dioxide to the atmosphere. It is a form of natural recycling (**Figure 67**).

Food chains are simplifications of what happens in reality. Most forms of food are eaten by more than one particular organism and **food webs** are better at showing the possible routes along which food may be transferred. **Figure 68** shows some of the possible

Figure 67

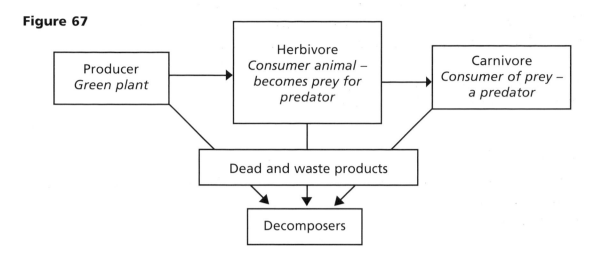

ways food – energy – flows through a pond ecosystem. Animals often have more than one source of food in their diets so a food web is a more accurate way of showing this. Note how the arrow heads show the direction in which the energy of the food flows through the ecosystem.

Figure 68

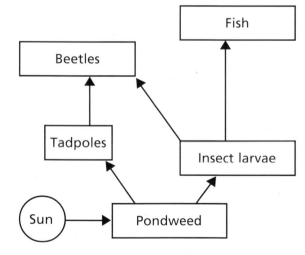

At each stage of transferring food energy, some energy is lost or dissipated from the system. For example some heat is lost following respiration of food at each link of the chain. This heat energy is not an available resource to the organism. In other words, animals at the end of the food chain have less energy available to them than animals near the beginning of the chain. This affects the numbers of organisms in a food chain. At the beginning of a food chain there will usually be greater numbers of living things than at the end of it. This can be represented as a **pyramid of numbers** (Figure 69).

Figure 69

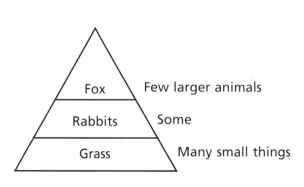

The numbers of living things decrease but the size or mass of individual organisms generally increases from the base to the top of the chain or pyramid model. Food chains can also be represented in a similar way using a **pyramid of biomass** that represents the mass of the living things at each part of the food chain.

Lesson focus: *Environment*

Early Learning Goals: *Knowledge and understanding of the world; Creative development*

KS1 NC Ref: *Sc2 5a*   **Year group:** *Reception*

Scheme of work unit: *2B – Plants and animals in the local environment*

Intended learning: for children to collect, observe and record observations of an invertebrate found in the outdoor environment.

Resources

❖ Magnispectors, plastic magnifying glasses, large paint brush, plastic collecting bottles, plastic insect, sponges, paint, paper, brushes, aprons, additional adult support if working outside the school boundary, CD ROM *Garden Wildlife* and computer.

❖ Plastic sweet jars, old fine mesh nylon.

Introduction: *Whole class session*

Read a story about an animal (e.g. *The Very Hungry Caterpillar*). Discuss what a caterpillar is. Explain that there are other animals in the school grounds and that an exploration should find some. Elicit children's ideas for working sensitively and safely with creatures. Show them collecting equipment and involve a child in helping to demonstrate how to collect from different places, using a plastic insect (e.g. to collect a ladybird gently use a paint brush to sweep it into a plastic container). Allocate any adult helpers to groups of children and prepare to go to collect.

On return to the classroom with their animals, help children to communicate:

❖ how they collected it;
❖ where they found it;
❖ what it looks like.

Introduce magnifying glasses for the children to observe the animals more closely. Ask questions which focus the children's attention on size, shape, colour, how it moves, where the legs are, special patterns, etc. They should wash their hands before the group activity.

Group or individual activities

Encourage children to make sponge print pictures of their animal. Use different shaped sponges and paint to make body outlines. For a ladybird the teacher can help them to choose a different shape for its head and body. The children choose red or orange paint to print the main part of the ladybird body and black for its head. They notice spots and legs on the body as they observe it again through a magnispector and they use a paint brush to add these to the print. With the teacher they use a book to find out other places where ladybirds can live. Use a CD ROM (e.g. *Garden Wildlife*) to show a video sequence of a ladybird feeding. They can add to their sponge print by painting the background to show where the animal lives.

Plenary session

Children show their prints of animals. A variety of animals has been studied and the teacher encourages the children to communicate what the animal is, where they found it, how they collected it sensitively, what they found out about where it lives and what it feeds on. The teacher can make a display of the children's prints and create a written set of questions to promote curiosity and encourage the children to think about other animals which they did not study. Use large plastic sweet jars to make three small vivaria (each with a different animal) for the display. Children are encouraged to go and observe the different animals and try to find answers to questions on display.

Points for assessment

❖ Can the children show you how to collect sensitively?
❖ Can they tell you the names of some animals in or near the school?
❖ Do they know where their particular animal lives, how it feeds and moves?

Teacher's own notes:

Lesson focus: *Environment*

KS1 NC Ref: *Sc1 1, 2a, b, e–h, j; Sc2 5b*   **Year group:** *Y1/2*

Scheme of work unit: *2B – Plants and animals in the local environment*

Intended learning: for children to know that a habitat is the place where something lives and that different habitats contain different living things.

Resources

❖ CD ROMs of different habitats (e.g. *Garden Wildlife* Anglia Multimedia), large photographs of different habitats (e.g. *Star Science Big Book*), ICT *My World* or *Survey*, computer and printer.

Introduction: *Whole class session*

Brainstorm a range of habitats near the school. List them on the board. Choose one habitat from the list and ask what it would be like to live there: what physical conditions would be experienced (e.g. dark, light, wet, dry)? Encourage them to predict which animals and plants might live in it. Co-ordinate class responses by listing them in a table on the board.

Habitat	What it is like	What we think lives there	What we found

Take children into the school grounds or local area with adult supervision which is compliant with school and LEA safety policy. Choose two areas (e.g. a hedgerow, wall, garden area, grassy area, school garden, pond, etc).

Group or individual activities

In groups in the outdoors, children draw the two different habitats they visit. They explore and draw more closely living things which they find in each and list and, if possible, count or estimate how many of each there were, e.g. dandelions: either a number or 'lots, many, few, none'. They note what each habitat was like, e.g. light, dark, damp, wet, etc. They wash their hands if animals and plants have been handled.

Plenary session

The groups share their findings. Co-ordinate which animals and plants the children found in each of the habitats and add this information to the table used initially to record elicitations prior to the visit. Encourage them to reflect on this evidence to see if their predictions were correct. Ask them how their data could be recorded and help them to see how a simple pictogram could be used to compare and contrast the most common animal and plant in each habitat (e.g. in the garden area they found three snails and ten dandelions; near the wall they found four woodlice and six groundsel plants). Sketch a pictogram of one set of results on the board.

Points for assessment

❖ Can the children name and describe two different habitats?
❖ Can they relate predictions to findings and speculate on differences?
❖ Can they consider and use information in tables and graphs?

Lesson focus: *Environment*

KS2 NC Ref: *Sc1 2a–c, e–j, l, m; Sc2 5b*   **Year group:** *Y3/4*

Scheme of work unit: *4B – Habitats*

Intended learning: for children to observe and measure some conditions in a local habitat that they have previously visited and to attempt to use the information creatively to explain why particular animals live in particular habitats.

Resources

❖ Soil/water measurer, light meter, thermostick thermometer.
❖ ICT opportunities: using sensors and data loggers; word processing.

Introduction: *Whole class session*

Revise habitats that children have recently visited and have some knowledge about the types of animals that live there. Use questions to focus on physical, qualitative (descriptive) conditions, e.g. light, dark.

Create an imaginary address for an animal that describes its environment and explain to the children that this is essentially what a habitat is:
For example:

Song Thrush
'By-the-Hedgerow'
Snailsville
Near South Meadow

The address could be used to give clues about what that particular animal prefers. Explain that the hedgerow provides shelter for the bird and that snails are its source of food. Any habitat should provide food and shelter for the animal.

Explain the task: to return to a nearby habitat and collect more information about it by measuring some of the conditions in it. This information will later be used to create an address for an animal or plant of their own choice which lives in the habitat to be visited. Children are to measure the soil temperature, soil moisture and light. Use a thermostick thermometer or soil thermometer. These are robust and will not break when placed in the soil. Involve a child in demonstrating how to do this using a plant-pot of soil. Show them how to read the scale. Introduce a soil water measurer. These are available from garden centres and have a simple colour coded scale from 1 to 4. Light blue is '1' and dark blue is '4'. Teach them how to use it and read the scale. Repeat with a light meter. If your school has a data logger this could be used with a computer, e.g. *Ecolog* or *First Sense*. Give the children a worksheet for recording information in a table e.g:

Name of habitat	Soil wetness	Soil temperature	Light reading

Take the children to a habitat ensuring adequate supervision and sensitivity for the habitat.

Group or individual activities

Groups take it in turns to share the equipment to take readings of water moisture, light, and temperature. The teacher checks that the children are reading the measuring scales and recording correctly. On returning to the classroom ensure they wash their hands.

Plenary session

Draw a large table on the board to collate group results. Encourage children to offer knowledge of what animals lived in the habitat and add this to the table. Help them to look for patterns in the evidence making connections to dampness, temperature and light. Children are then asked to imagine that they are an animal in this habitat and to write to another animal in a different habitat explaining why they like to live in their own habitat and not that of the animal to which they are writing. This encourages them to create an address for 'themselves' and one for the animal to whom they are writing (e.g. it could be a snail writing to a thrush or a worm writing to a snail). This supports and relates directly to the National Literacy Project for Year 4 Term 3 on 'Writing Composition – writing in the form of a letter'. Later in the week the children share their letters and some are re-drafted on the computer for class display.

Points for assessment

❖ Can the children explain a habitat?
❖ Can the children use equipment to measure physical aspects of the habitat?
❖ Do they know why certain animals are suited to certain environments?

Teacher's own notes:

Lesson focus: *Environment*

KS2 NC Ref: *Sc2 5e*   **Year group:** *Y5/6*

Scheme of work unit: *6A – Interdependence and adaptation*

Intended learning: for children to know examples of food chains and understand the feeding relationships they represent, in terms of producer, consumer, predator and prey.

Resources

❖ Big Book pictures of habitats, PE bands, paper clips.

❖ A set of cards to include words and pictures of the Sun, a green water plant, a mayfly, a caddis larva, a beetle, a salmon.

Introduction: *Whole class session*

Use large pictures or videos of animals in habitats to discuss how living things feed and what they depend on. Elicit some foods that children had for their last meal. Ask where it came from and for each answer add an overriding question, 'and where from before that?' You should end up with green plants! Explain that green plants make food using sunlight and we call them producers. Animals that eat plants are consumers and an animal that eats another animal is a predator and its food is its prey. Use a big book picture of a pond to further explain these points and make diagrams of some food chains in the pond. In this lesson the whole class will be engaged in food chain games in the school hall. It could be part of PE time.

Group or individual activities

Game 1: Plant and animal relationship game

Each child wears a PE band and needs a paper clip. The teacher issues each child with a card. It is fixed on to the front of the PE band with the clip. Children then have to move around freely, imagining they are living in a pond.

When they get a signal (e.g. whistle), they form a linear food chain as fast as possible. It must start with the Sun and end with the biggest animal of the set. It has to be in order of Sun (the source of the energy), producers (a green water plant), consumer/herbivore (a mayfly), small predator (a caddis larva), medium sized predator (beetle) and largest predator (a salmon).

Game 2: Upsetting the balance

A. Play this game using the same cards as before omitting the Sun and green plant, but make only two children in the class salmon. Use a red PE band for the salmon, green for beetle, yellow for caddis and blue for mayfly to allocate the rest of the class to a role. Every time a child is tagged by a salmon, they drop out and count to 15, then rejoin the game. Do the salmon ever manage to 'eat' all the animals?

B. Find out what happens as the number of salmon increase to four by playing the same game. If tagged by a salmon, drop out, count to 15 then rejoin the game. How does the number of animals change? Is it harder to keep the same numbers of first and second consumers?

C. Repeat the game with eight salmon and then 16 salmon. What happens to the food of the salmon? Will the salmon survive?

Plenary session

The teacher discusses the results of the games with the children, using questions such as:

- ❖ 'What do living things in habitats have to do to ensure that they survive?'
- ❖ 'What happens if one group of animals consumes food faster than it can be replaced?'

Children draw and write about food chains using scientific language and arrows to represent the direction in which food moves along the chain. Some children are encouraged to research about other food chains and create a similar game for the class to play.

Points for assessment

- ❖ Can the children explain a food chain?
- ❖ Can they give an example of a food chain and draw it schematically?
- ❖ Do they know the meaning of the terms producer, predator, consumer, prey?
- ❖ Do they know that food chains begin with green plants?

Teacher's own notes:

Chapter 9
Forces

Teachers need personal knowledge of:

▲ what a force is;
▲ types of forces;
▲ measuring force;
▲ how to represent forces diagrammatically;
▲ speeding up and slowing down;
▲ friction;
▲ floating and sinking.

Forces

A force is a **push** or **pull**. A push force moves objects away from you and a pull force moves objects towards you. Forces make things move, speed up, slow down, change direction and stop. Forces can change the shape of materials. When modelling with Plasticine, pushes and pulls are used to change its shape.

Variations on pushes or pulls are bends and twists. If you bend a ruler it is a push force. If you put a screw into a piece of wood, you apply a twisting push force. If you unscrew it you apply a twisting force which is a pull force. Children can push and pull toys with wheels, e.g. pram, pedal car. Think about how many times you use forces – pushes and pulls – in a kitchen or other parts of the home.

For an object to move in a certain direction there has to be a bigger force in that direction. To lift a book from the table, the upward force must be bigger than the pull down force of **gravity**. Gravity is a force that is exerted between all objects but it is only noticeable when there is a large difference in size or mass between objects (see **Figure 70**).

The Earth is massive and exerts a huge pull down force on all objects. This is the Earth's force of gravity that keeps everything on the Earth's surface and this pull force is directed towards the centre of the Earth.

The gravitational pull on an object is the object's weight and is measured in **Newtons**. In school we use Newton meters or forcemeters to measure force and therefore weight. These meters look like spring balances. A mass of one kilogram has a weight of about 10 Newtons.

When objects are not moving there are balanced forces acting on them. A stationary football on a field has two forces acting on it: gravity pulls down and the ground pushes back with an

Figure 70

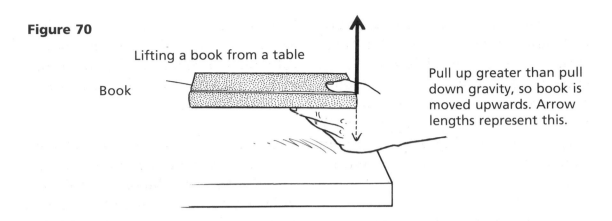

Lifting a book from a table

Book

Pull up greater than pull down gravity, so book is moved upwards. Arrow lengths represent this.

equal but opposite force, so the ball does not move. Forces always act in pairs (**Figure 71**).

Figure 71

Push up and pull down forces on the ball are balanced, so it does not move. Both arrows are the same length, representing equal forces.

Forces and movement

Objects move when force is applied. Forces make things speed up, slow down, change direction and stop. **Speed** is how far an object moves in a certain unit of time (**Figure 72**).

Figure 72

$$\text{Speed} = \frac{\text{Distance}}{\text{Time}}$$

It is usually measured in metres per second or miles per hour. If the speed of the object changes by either going faster, slowing down or stopping the object is **accelerating**. **Velocity** is a term used to indicate the direction in which an object is moving. A car travelling from London to Leeds on the M1 at 60 mph would be travelling at a velocity of 60 mph north. Thus velocity is speed in a given direction.

If a marble is rolled across the floor it begins to slow down and stop. There is a force between the surfaces of the floor and the marble that tries to stop it moving. This is **friction** (**Figure 73**).

Friction

Figure 73

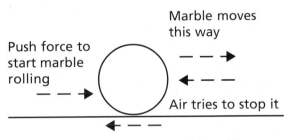

Push force to start marble rolling

Marble moves this way

Air tries to stop it

Friction tries to stop marble rolling

Friction exists between any two surfaces. If you rub your hands together, the friction that tries to stop movement manifests itself as heat. When car brakes are applied, friction is being used to stop the movement. Friction between the soles of shoes and the floor resists movement. To apply friction is less easy in icy conditions. The greater the depth of tread or pattern on shoes and tyres the greater the friction between the two surfaces and the less likelihood of falling or skidding. Parachutes also make use of friction of **air resistance** that slows down the movement. When things speed up, friction forces increase. When driving a car, friction between the road and tyres and from the air tend to resist movement. By varying the driving force to meet conditions the car can be maintained at a steady speed.

When objects of different masses are dropped from the same point, they will land at the same time unless air resistance on them is different. Similar shape and size objects will experience the same air resistance and reach the ground at the same time. If however two different materials are used, the one that experiences the most air resistance will reach the ground last, e.g. a kilogram of feathers will not reach the ground in the same time as a kilogram of lead because the feathers take up more space and experience more air resistance than the same mass of lead (**Figure 74**). In a vacuum the rate at which objects fall towards the ground is the same.

Figure 74

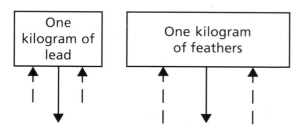

The force due to gravity is the same on both objects but air resistance – friction – is greater on the feathers.

Floating, sinking and density

The **density** of a material will determine if it floats or sinks in water.

Density depends on how tightly particles are packed in a given space or volume. The amount of material in a piece of substance is known as that substance's **mass**.

Mass, unlike weight, does not change. For example if a kilogram of lead was transported to the Moon it would still have the same amount of matter or 'stuff' in it; its mass would be unchanged. On Earth it would weigh 1.0 Newton. However, its **weight** would be different because weight is due to the pull down force of gravity on the material. The Earth is six times more massive than the Moon. The Moon exerts a pull force that is one sixth as big as that on Earth. Therefore the lead would weigh only 0.16 Newtons on the Moon even though it has the same amount of matter on both the Moon and the Earth.

The **density** of an object is the amount of material in a unit volume. For example 100 grams of water has a volume of 100cm^3. Therefore, every gram occupies one cubic centimetre (**Figure 75**).

Figure 75

Density = $\dfrac{\text{Mass}}{\text{Volume}}$

$\dfrac{100}{100}$ = 1.00 gram per cubic centimetre often written 1g^{-1} cm^{-3}

Materials that have more than one gram of matter in a cubic centimetre of the material will be more dense than water and so will not float in water but **sink**. Materials that have less than one gram of matter in a cubic centimetre will be less dense than water and so will **float**.

Water expands at freezing point so there is more space for every gram of the particles. This makes the density of ice less than one gram per cubic centimetre, and so it floats on the liquid water.

It is possible to change the shape of materials that sink. For example a ball of Plasticine sinks. If its shape is changed into a boat shape, then air is introduced into the 'hull' of the material. The material now has a larger volume and has had air introduced into it. There is now less than one gram of material – air plus Plasticine – for every cubic centimetre of volume the shape occupies, so its density has fallen. When the density of the Plasticine boat shape becomes less than one gram per cubic centimetre the shape will float on water.

Real and apparent weight and upthrust

If an object, e.g. half a house brick, is suspended from a Newton meter in air, you are measuring its weight in air. If the object is then lowered so that it is immersed in water, its weight appears to change. This is because the pull down force on the object is less due to the push up on it from the water. The push up force from the water is the **upthrust**. The value of the upthrust is the difference between the object's weight in air and water.

Upthrust can be experienced by pushing an empty plastic bottle with a screw top lid down into the water and then releasing it. The upthrust pushes the bottle to the surface where it floats. Objects float when the upthrust from the water is equal to the weight of the object. If the upthrust is less than the weight of the object it will sink. This is the basis of Archimedes' principle which states that when an object is immersed in a fluid, it experiences an upthrust equal to the weight of fluid displaced.

Lesson focus: *Forces*

Early Learning Goal: *Knowledge and understanding of the world*

KS1 NC Ref: *Sc4 2b*   **Year group:** *Reception*

Scheme of work unit: *1E – Pushes and pulls*

Intended learning: For children to know that a force is a push or pull and to be able to use these words accurately.

Resources
- Pictures of things moving, e.g. a children's playground, a fun fair, a winter sports scene.
- A big toy, e.g. a car or lorry.
- A 'push' 'pull' clown puppet.
- Sets of printed labels/flash cards for 'push' and 'pull' with a picture symbol for each word.
- Blu-tack.

Introduction: *Whole class session*

Play a word game. Brainstorm the word 'force' and ask children what they think of when they hear the word 'force'. Many will associate this with the social meaning of being 'made to do something' by an older person, e.g. 'Mum forced me to go to bed early'. Introduce a large picture which has lots of 'movement' in it. Ask children which things they think are moving. List them. Then discuss how these things were made to move. This may elicit the terms 'push' and 'pull'. If not, teach the words and explain their meaning. A toy stick puppet may help (e.g. a clown in a 'cone' – push the stick to make the clown's head appear; pull to move the clown's head into the cone).

Use flash cards of each word with a symbol, e.g. of a closed hand for pull and a flat hand for push. Then introduce a big toy which has wheels and a piece of string on the front end. Ask the children how they could move the toy and let some children demonstrate their ideas to others. Check that the children are using push for moving the car away from them and pull for moving the car towards them. Repeat using another object, e.g. empty box, and give instructions for push and pull.

Group or individual activities

In small groups children look around the classroom for objects that can be moved safely by pushing and pulling. (Do not allow them to move electrical equipment or other unstable things in the room.) They stick force labels on them. Intervene to check their understanding of the words.

Plenary session

The children share some of their ideas of things they pushed and pulled. To reinforce their understanding use a different Big Book picture and ask children to stick a push or pull word using Blu-tack onto objects they think might be moving. Discuss some objects that can be pushed and pulled. Children then draw and write to show two of their favourite push objects and two of their favourite pull objects.

Points for assessment
- Do the children know what push and pull mean?
- Can they use the words scientifically?

Lesson focus: *Forces*

KS1 NC Ref: *Sc1 1, 2b, e–h, j; Sc4 2c*   **Year group:** *Y1/2*

Scheme of work unit: *2E – Forces and movement*

Intended learning: for children to know that forces can make things speed up, slow down or change direction and to record and consider evidence using a table.

Resources

❖ Water tray, toy sailing boat – could be made from small margarine tub, dowel and card sail.
❖ Sand timer or stop clock.
❖ Dowelling, Plasticine, battery hand-held fan or balloon pump.

Safety! Do not use a mains fan or hairdryer.

Introduction: *Whole class session*

Ask the children if they have seen yachts sailing. Show a picture if possible. Talk about how sailing boats move and what and where the force comes from to make them move. Ask some children to show how they can move the boat in the water tray. Ask them when sailing boats would move fast or slow. Do they make connections with wind speed? Do they know that sailing boats can change direction? If not, show them using the model boat in the water tray. Set up challenges for children to make the boats:

❖ sail fast;
❖ sail slow;
❖ change directions as many times as possible along a slalom course in the water tray using dowel with numbered flags and Plasticine. The boats have to zigzag around the course.

Group or individual activities

Children try the challenges. Intervene to ensure correct language is used, e.g. 'speed up', 'slow down', 'change direction'. Encourage children to make up the rules for the slalom course. Support their recording by designing a table for them to complete, e.g:

Number of flags	Time in seconds (or judgement for differentiated recording, e.g. slow, fast, very fast)
2	10 seconds (fast) etc.
3	
4	
5	
6	

Plenary session

Discuss the challenges with the children. Children explain how they made the boat go slower. Help the children make a connection as to how far away the fan or wind force was from the boat. The groups that recorded the times for the slalom race in a two column table explain how they changed the position of the hand-held battery fan to change the direction of movement of the boat. Help the class interpret the tables of results for the slalom race using questions which focus on how the number of flags affects the time it takes to complete the course. Children draw and write about how a force can speed up, slow down or change the direction of the boat. For homework, ask children to make up and play a game with a parent or carer which also involves changing the speed and direction of movement of a different object (e.g. blow football). Follow this up at a later time.

Points for assessment

❖ Do the children know that some things can be made to speed up, slow down and change direction?
❖ Do they know how this can be done for a sail boat?
❖ Can they spot how forces can speed up, slow down or change the direction of objects?
❖ Can they use a table, with teacher support, to record their measurements?
❖ Can they interpret their evidence?

Teacher's own notes:

Lesson focus: *Forces*

KS2 NC Ref: *Sc1 1b, 2a–m, Sc4 2c–e*   **Year group:** *Y3/4*

Scheme of work unit: *4E – Friction*

Intended learning: for children to apply their knowledge of friction by planning and carrying out an investigation to find which type of shoe gives the best grip.

Resources

❖ Two or three different types/brands of training shoes.
❖ Newton meters (force meter/spring balance) 0-1N, 0-5N, 0-10N.
❖ Planning boards (e.g. from *Star Science* junior books).
❖ Two hair brushes.

Introduction: *Whole class session*

Revise with the children the concept of friction (the force which tries to stop two objects moving over each other). Illustrate the idea of friction with two hair brushes moving over each other in opposite directions, noting what happens to the bristles. The notion of friction should be taught before any investigations about friction. Ask the children which type of trainer would give the best grip on the playground. How could they find out? Discuss some ideas offered in order to focus groups on the challenge. Use a planning structure, e.g. planning board, to scaffold the key points. For example, question:

❖ What we will change:
❖ What we will measure:
❖ What we will keep the same to make a fair test:
❖ Our results table will look like this:
❖ Equipment we need:

Group or individual activities

Children plan and carry out their investigation. Some children place each trainer on the same surface, e.g. lino covered area of the room. Then they choose a force meter from a range of those available which enables them to measure the force needed to start the trainer moving and overcome friction. They record this and repeat with another trainer. Intervene to ask why one trainer has a better grip than the other. Children look at the soles and note that the pattern is different. They decide to modify their recording table format by adding another column and drawing part of the shoe pattern, counting and recording the number of ridges across the widest part of the shoe as well. Their table looked like this:

Make of trainer	Force to overcome friction (Newtons)	Pattern of trainer & number of ridges across widest part

Plenary session

Ask groups to share their results. Draw a table on the board and co-ordinate the sharing of evidence. The one group which noticed pattern difference shares its results last. A separate table is drawn for them. Use questions such as:

❖ How many trainers did they use?
❖ Which one took the biggest force to move it?
❖ Which one took the smallest force to move it?
❖ Which trainer would give the best grip on the playground?
❖ Does the pattern on the sole make a difference to the grip?
❖ How does it make a difference?

Discuss how these results could be drawn as a bar graph.

Children note that the sole with the most ridges also gave the best grip but they were uncertain because the trainers had been worn for different lengths of time. They suggest only new trainers could give reliable evidence by making the test really fair.

Points for assessment

❖ Do the children know what friction is and that force meters measure it?
❖ Could they plan, with support, their investigation?
❖ Did they decide what to measure?
❖ Can they explain why a test is fair or unfair?
❖ Can they record in a table?
❖ Can they identify trends in results and use them to check initial predictions and make conclusions?

Teacher's own notes:

Lesson focus: *Forces*

KS2 NC Ref: *Sc1 1b; 2b, e, f, h–j, l; Sc4 2d, 2e*   **Year group:** *Y5/6*

Scheme of work unit: *6E – Forces in action*

Intended learning: for children to know that if something floats there are balanced forces acting on it and that the pull down force due to gravity equals the push up force – upthrust – from the water.

Resources

❖ Plastic tanks, force meters (spring balances), range of objects which float, e.g. plastic pop bottles, balls, inflated balloon and some that sink, e.g. paper clip, stone.

Introduction: *Whole class session*

A lead into this concept could be made by referring to a tug of war in a previous PE lesson. Use the experience to discuss when the rope was moved and when it was not moved using the terms 'balanced' and 'unbalanced' forces. On the board, draw the effect of the forces, using different sized arrows to represent the size and direction of the pull forces in the tug of war. Now place an empty plastic pop bottle (with its top on) in a plastic aquarium of water. Note how it floats and that it is not moving. Discuss the pull down force due to gravity. Ask one child to push the bottle down into the water and hold it there. Explain that when it is not moving there are balanced forces on it. Ask what will happen if the child lets go of the bottle. Try it and see. The water pushes the bottle to the surface. Explain that at the surface the 'push up' from the water is now equal to the 'pull down' from the bottle and it does not move. Use this to present the group activity which is to find out if other objects behave in similar ways and then measure and record the force on objects when floating in water using a force meter calibrated in Newtons (N).

Group or individual activities

Children try out their tests. They use a force meter to measure the 'weight' force on the object when floating. They record these measurements in a table.

Object	Force when floating (N)
Ball	
Empty bottle without lid,	
etc	

Plenary session

Discuss the results. Draw a table on the board and co-ordinate the sharing of results. A pattern emerges suggesting that when objects are floating their weight is zero. Ask a child to draw a 'floating object' on the board. Use arrows to show that the forces are balanced and make both arrows the same size. Explain that when the object is balanced the water pushing up is balanced by the weight of the object being pulled down. When an object does not float the weight (pull force due to gravity) of the object is greater than the upward pushing force from the water. Discuss and explain how to represent this idea with arrows of different sizes. Children reinforce their learning by choosing objects that floated from their results and drawing diagrams with arrows to show the size of balanced forces. They explain in writing using scientific terms: push, pull upthrust, gravity, float, underlining each term in colour as they use it.

Points for assessment

❖ Do the children know that when something is not moving there are balanced forces acting on it?
❖ Do they know that when something is floating the push up from the water equals the pull down force (weight) of the object?
❖ Can they explain this in terms of balanced forces?
❖ Can they represent forces in diagrams using arrows?

Teacher's own notes:

Chapter 10
Earth and beyond

The Earth is a minute part of the **universe**. The universe includes everything that exists and is a huge concept to grasp. Scientists currently explain how the universe may have originated in their big bang theory. This theory is predicated on the idea a 'big bang' occurred about 15 million years ago and created matter. Subsequently matter moved into structures to create **stars** which then grew old and exploded, spreading matter further into the universe so that it could be used to create new stars and planets. However, this idea may not match existing religious beliefs of some people. In the future, scientists may gain further evidence that may lead to a re-interpretation and different explanations of the origin of the universe.

Major components of the universe are **galaxies**. Galaxies are vast groups of stars held in place by gravity. When the sky is observed at night, the stars we see are only a few of the billions in our particular galaxy that is known as the **Milky Way**. It is called the Milky Way because from our planet Earth it looks like a band of milky light that is brightest in the centre and becomes dimmer towards its extremities. This galaxy rotates slowly turning once approximately every 200 million years.

The Milky Way is a **spiral galaxy** because it looks like a rotating wheel of stars that has the coolest red stars at its centre and hotter 'blue' stars in its outer parts which are known as 'arms'. It is in the arms of spiral galaxies that new stars will form from gas and dust.

Irregular galaxies have no particular shape. The smallest galaxies contain about 100,000 stars and the largest known galaxies about 3,000 billion stars. Groups of stars make patterns or **constellations**, e.g. The Plough. In the northern hemisphere Polaris, the North Pole Star, seems to stay in the same place as the Earth rotates (**Figure 76**).

Figure 76

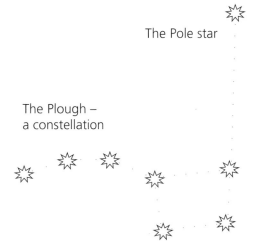

The Pole star

The Plough – a constellation

Stars have visual surface colour features that are determined by their surface temperature. Stars, such as our **Sun**, generate heat and light and other forms of energy that make up the **electromagnetic spectrum**. This energy results from atomic nuclear particles of hydrogen fusing to make helium, and as they fuse vast amounts of energy are released.

Star colour	Surface temperature °C
Red	3,500
Yellow	6,000
Blue	50,000

Our nearest star is the Sun. It is 150 million kilometres away from Earth. The Sun appears to be yellow and is a medium hot star with a surface temperature of 6,000 °C and a central core temperature of about 15 million °C. Magnetic effects on the Sun's surface cause **sunspots** and then spectacular solar flares occur. These can interfere with modern terrestrial communication systems and occur about every 11 years. Scientists estimate that the Sun is half way through its life. They predict it will last for another 5 million years and then it will grow bigger, cooler and develop into a cooler red star. As it grows bigger, scientists predict that it will swallow up our planet Earth before shrinking and cooling to a cold brown shell.

Safety! When children are studying the Sun they must be told never to look directly at it: it can cause permanent damage to the eyes. Only approved safety viewers should be used to observe an eclipse. A safe way to observe the Sun is to project its image onto a screen through binoculars or telescopes.

The solar system and length of a planet's year

Our **solar system** includes all the **planets** that orbit our nearest star – the Sun. The word 'planet' means wanderer. Planets and their moons are not light sources. They all receive light from the Sun and reflect it. When we see our Moon we see sunlight that has been reflected from it. Each planet spins on its axis as it orbits the Sun. The time a planet takes to spin once on its axis is a **day** and to make one orbit of the Sun is a **year**.

The length of a day and year therefore varies for each planet because they are all at different distances from the Sun. Pluto is the planet furthest from the Sun and it takes 248.6 equivalent Earth years to orbit the Sun once. Each planet rotates on its axis once during that planet's day. The table on page 105 shows the relative length of each planet's day in terms of Earth days. The Earth orbits the Sun once every 365.25 days. In most years we use 365 days but every four years an extra day is included to make a **leap year**.

There are nine known planets in the solar system. These, in order of increasing distance from the Sun, are **Mercury, Venus, Earth, Mars, Jupiter, Saturn, Uranus, Neptune** and **Pluto**. Children may find the following mnemonic useful for remembering the names and order from the Sun:

My Very Easy Method Just Shows U Nine Planets.

The four innermost planets, Mercury, Venus, Earth and Mars are made of rock, and the next four – Jupiter, Saturn, Uranus and Neptune – are made of gases, mostly hydrogen and helium. Pluto is made of rock and ice.

The Sun is the biggest body in the solar system. It has more mass than the rest of the solar system and so exerts enormous gravitational forces on the planets. This huge force keeps the planets in place and makes them orbit the Sun.

Some planets have naturally occurring **satellites** that orbit them. These are called moons. All planets except Mercury and Venus have one or more moons (See **Figure 77** overleaf).

The Moon

Our Moon is a satellite of the Earth. It is our nearest neighbour in space but only about a quarter the size of the Earth. Its smaller mass means that it exerts a smaller force of gravity than the Earth. Gravity on the Moon is one sixth of that on Earth. The Moon is 384,400km (238,906 miles) away. There is no man on the Moon, even

Planet	Distance from Sun (millions of km)	Temperature range °C	Time for one orbit of Sun – a year	Time to rotate once	Material	Number of moons
Mercury	58	-170 – 350	88 days	59 Earth days	Rock	0
Venus	105	465	225 days	243 Earth days	Rock	0
Earth (only planet with lots of water)	150	22	1 year	1 Earth day	Rock	1
Mars	228	-23	1.9 years	1 Earth day	Rock	2
Jupiter	780	-150	12 years	10 Earth hours (0.42 Earth days)	Liquid hydrogen & helium	16
Saturn	1,430	-180	29 years	10 Earth hours (0.42 Earth days)	Hydrogen & helium	17
Uranus	2,870	-210	84 years	17 – 28 Earth hours	Ice, hydrogen & helium	15
Neptune	4,500	-220	165 years	16 – 20 Earth hours	Ice, hydrogen & helium	8
Pluto	5,900	-220	248 years	6 Earth days	Ice & rock	1

Figure 77

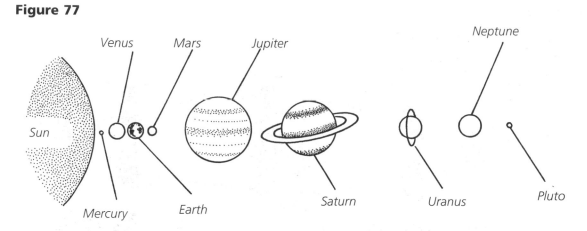

though a full Moon appears to have a man's face. Dark lowland areas and brighter mountainous areas cause these apparent 'facial' features. The Moon reflects light from the Sun. It is not a light source.

Phases of the Moon

The Moon has a cycle of 27 days 7 hours. That is known as a lunar month. This is the time it takes for the Moon to orbit the Earth once, and as it does so it rotates only once. However, because the Earth is also orbiting the Sun it takes 29.5 days to return to the same phase.

Each night the Moon seems to change its shape. It grows bigger – **waxes** – as it moves to become a full Moon – or grows smaller – **wanes** – as it moves towards a crescent shape again from being a full Moon. The changes in shape are known as **phases** of the Moon. The apparent change in shape of the Moon is explained by the changing daily position of the Moon in relation to the Sun and Earth with the illuminated part of the Moon changing daily.

At about the time of a new Moon the unlit side of the Moon faces the Earth.

The Moon is then not visible from Earth. As it begins to orbit the Earth, parts of the side lit by sunlight become visible. By day eight it is a half Moon and at the first quarter phase with the **right side** of the Moon visible. Waxing continues to day 15 when it is a full Moon and we see all the sunlit side that faces the Earth.

By day 22 the Moon is at the last phase or last quarter and waning and the **left side** is visible. The same side of the Moon is always visible to us because the Moon spins on its axis at the same rate that it orbits the Earth (**Figure 78**).

Eclipses

There are two kinds of **eclipse** that we experience on Earth: **lunar** eclipse and **solar** eclipse. Lunar eclipse occur when a full Moon is slowly covered by a shadow of the Earth. The Earth, Moon and Sun have to be fully aligned so that the Earth blocks light from the Sun and this creates a shadow of the Earth that is cast onto the Moon. This causes the Moon to look a coppery-red colour that is caused by light refracted through the Earth's atmosphere.

Solar eclipses are formed when the Moon passes between the Earth and

Figure 78

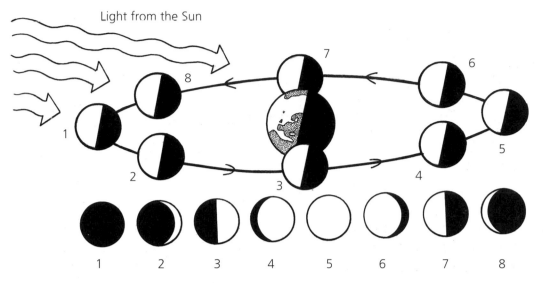

the Sun blocking out the Sun. If the eclipse is total, the outer part of the Sun – the **corona** – can be seen as a pearly white halo on the edge of a black disc of the eclipsed Sun. The total eclipse can only last for short periods of time from 20 seconds to 7 minutes 31 seconds. The shadow of the total eclipse of the Sun on August 11 1999 crossed the Atlantic Ocean in 40 minutes, and travelled over Cornwall and Devon in 2 minutes 6 seconds, before moving on to parts of Europe, North Africa and western Asia.

As the Moon passes between the Sun and the Earth it casts a dark shadow – the **umbra** – on part of the Earth (**Figure 79**). Any area of the Earth in the dark shadow will see a **total eclipse** because none of the light from the Sun can be observed within this shadow. The lighter part of the shadow, the **penumbra**, will see only a **partial eclipse** because not all the light from the Sun is blocked by the Moon at these points. Because the Earth and Moon are moving, the dark umbral shadow travels quickly from east to west across the face of the

Earth. All parts of the Earth in this umbral shadow will have the chance to witness a total eclipse because they lie in the path of totality.

Figure 79

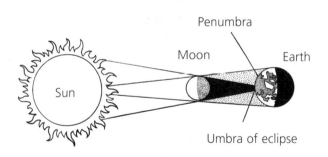

Night and day

A day is the time it takes for the Earth to rotate (spin) once; one rotation takes 24 hours. The Earth rotates in an anticlockwise direction from west to east and so the Sun rises in the east and sets in the west. When the part of the Earth we are on faces the Sun it is day and when it is not facing the Sun it is night. The rotation of the Earth makes the Sun appear to move across the sky from east to west (**Figure 80**). During

Figure 80

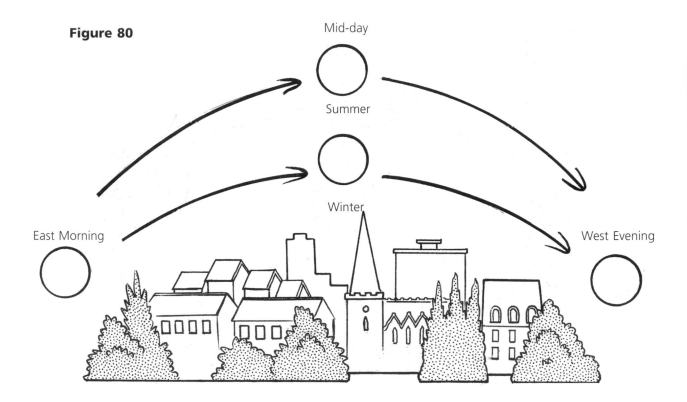

Mid-day

Summer

Winter

East Morning

West Evening

a day the Sun is lowest in the sky at sunrise and sunset. At midday on June 21 it reaches its highest point. The Sun appears to be lower in the sky in winter.

When it is day in Britain it is night in America. American time is behind British time. This is because the Earth rotates from west to east. Countries east of Britain have time that is ahead of ours.

Remember! Ḙast is Ḟast.

Seasons of the year

The Earth is tilted on its axis. The axis is an imaginary line that passes through the north and south poles. This axis is tilted at 23.5^0 from the vertical. This causes different amounts of light and therefore heat, to reach different parts of the Earth at different times of the year resulting in the seasons of the year. NB all parts of the Earth received the same amount of light over a year.

When the northern part of the Earth is tilted towards the Sun, it is summer in the northern hemisphere. Days are long and nights are short. Inside the Arctic Circle the Sun never sets at the height of summer, hence the term 'land of the midnight Sun' (**Figure 81**).

In the northern hemisphere the longest day is June 21; also known as the summer solstice. The Sun will appear at it highest point in the sky at midday on June 21 as the Earth reaches its halfway point in its journey round the Sun. As the Earth travels toward the opposite side of the Sun tilting away from it, autumn begins, followed by winter.

Figure 81

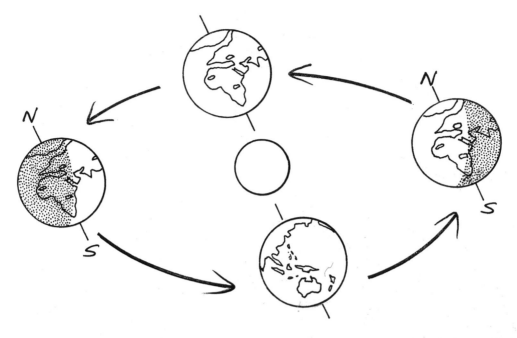

Other key dates for the northern hemisphere in the Earth's journey round the Sun are shown in the table below.

Date	Event
June 21	*Summer solstice* – the longest day
September 21	*Autumn equinox* – day and night equal
December 21	*Winter solstice* – the shortest day
March 21	*Spring equinox* – day and night equal

Lesson focus: *Earth and beyond*

Early Learning Goals: *Knowledge and understanding of the world;
Creative Development; Language and Literacy*

KS1 NC Ref: *Sc4 3a, b*   **Year group:** *Reception*

Scheme of work unit: *Links to 1D and 5E*

Intended learning: for children to become aware that there are stars and planets in the sky/space;
to know that astronauts have to take food, air and water on their expeditions.

Resources

❖ Old blackout curtains and a table to make a very dark place for an imaginary space journey.
❖ One set of 'glow in the dark planets and Quasar stars'.
❖ Torches.
❖ Large pictures of the Earth and other planets, e.g. *Star Science* Big Book pp 30–32.
❖ Dressing-up clothes for role playing astronauts.
❖ Globe.
❖ Toy or old radio.
❖ Books about space.
❖ Paper, paint and brushes.

Introduction: *Whole class session*

Discuss children's ideas of what they think the Earth is like. Children may have difficulty
understanding the Earth is round like a sphere and not round like a dinner plate. Show pictures of
the Earth (taken from space) and astronauts and talk about them. Use a globe to develop the idea
that the Earth is a sphere. Explain that the picture was taken from a rocket sent into space. Use this
as the context for the activity. What would they need to take with them to stay alive? (Air, food,
water, special shiny clothes that reflect the Sun's energy, some of which is harmful; gloves, radio for
keeping in touch with Earth, etc.) Explain that in small groups they will go on a journey into space.
They need to choose their clothing and materials to take with them. The dark place is outer space
where they will be able to see stars and planets and these will glow. (The teacher fixes these in
position under the table before the activity with Blu-tack.) They can use torches to help them spot
the planets. Children are challenged to see how many planets (up to nine) and stars they can spot
and what they are like, and have to report back either by pretend radio with an Earth station or
when they return to whole group session at the end.

Group or individual activities

In small groups the children dress up, decide what to take and go on their 'space journey'. They
shine their torches to see what they can find and talk about the colours and sizes of the planets and
stars.

Plenary session

Review the learning by encouraging them to share their experiences. Use questions such as:
❖ Could you see the stars and planets?
❖ Which were the easiest to see?
❖ How were the planets different in shape to the stars?
❖ Were the planets all the same size?

After questioning, show the planets that had been in 'space'. Ask if anyone knows the names of
some planets. Show the children the writing on the back of the 'planets' and write them on the

board. (Mars, Pluto, Mercury, Venus, Uranus, Saturn, Jupiter, Earth and Neptune.) Explain that even though the planets are a long way from Earth, the stars are much further away and, like the Sun, all stars are very, very hot. Later some children paint pictures of planets for display after researching details in books.

Points for assessment

❖ Can the children distinguish between stars and planets in their role play?
❖ Do they have ideas about what to wear and what to take on a space journey?
❖ Can they talk about their expedition and do they know the names of some planets?

Teacher's own notes:

Lesson focus: *Earth and beyond*

KS1 NC Ref: *Sc4 3a, b*   **Year group:** *Y1/2*

Scheme of work unit: *1D – Light and dark*

Intended learning: for children to know that the Sun is a source of light for the Earth and if light from the Sun is blocked it goes darker; to know that it is dangerous to look directly at the Sun.

Resources

❖ A sunny day with moving clouds!
❖ Yellow card – shaped like the Sun and grey cloud shapes (5) collectively big enough to cover the Sun.
❖ Paper, paint and brushes.
❖ Pictures of the Sun and the effect of a lunar eclipse.

Introduction: *Whole class session*

Ask children where the Sun is and what they think it is made of. List their ideas on the board. Ask them to think what it would be like if we did not have a Sun and then list their ideas. Show photographs of the Sun and discuss them. Explain that they are going into the playground to find out what happens when the Sun goes in (i.e. when it goes behind a cloud). It is very important for children to learn not to look directly at the Sun because it can damage their eyes. They should be told this before moving onto the playground. On the playground tell the children to find a place and stand so that the Sun is behind them. Ask them to raise an arm when they think a cloud passes in front of the Sun and lower it when the Sun is fully shining. Scan the playground to see if arms are raised and lowered at the correct time. Ask the children how they knew when to adopt the correct procedure and what was formed on the playground when the cloud passed in front of the Sun. (Shadow formed.) Ask the children what causes a shadow to form. (Sunlight being blocked by a cloud.) Explain that this change is not the same as nightfall because the Sun is still shining even when behind a cloud. Challenge the children to make as many shadow shapes as they can on their own, in pairs and small groups.

Group or individual activities

Children explore making shadows. The teacher observes and intervenes to support children as necessary. Teacher observations and intervention in the group's activities are used for discussion in the plenary session.

If the Sun does not shine, try this. Choose one child to be the Sun and give him or her a cardboard cut-out of the Sun to hold against the chest. Choose, say, five children and give each a large, grey cloud shape. Ask the class to look at the child who is the Sun. Ask why they can see the 'Sun'. (No clouds in front of it.) Then ask the children with 'clouds' to stand in front of the Sun. Ask the class why they cannot now see the Sun. Let other groups play this to reinforce the idea that the Sun is a source of light for the Earth and if light from the Sun is blocked it goes darker.

Plenary session

Ask children what shapes of shadow they made and some demonstrate their shadows to the class. Ask the class to carefully observe the shadows that are made and to offer suggestions for making better shadow shapes and investigating more about the Sun and shadows. Back in the classroom, ask if anyone knows what happens when there is an eclipse. Show pictures of the effect of an eclipse in Cornwall on August 11 1999. This is used to help the children make the connection that when the Sun is completely blocked by the Moon it creates a shadow on part of the Earth so it becomes very dark for a short time.

Children draw some of the shadow shapes they made and write a sentence about how shadows and clouds block light. Some children also make posters to stop people looking directly at the Sun for display in the school.

Points for assessment
❖ Do the children know that the Sun is the source of light for the Earth?
❖ Do they know that clouds stop some light reaching the Earth?
❖ Do they know that it is harmful to look directly at the Sun?

Teacher's own notes:

Lesson focus: *Earth and beyond*

KS2 NC Ref: *Sc1 1b, 2a–c, e, f, h–j, l, m; Sc4 4b*　　　　**Year group:** *Y3/4*

Scheme of work unit: *3F – Light and shadows*

Intended learning: for children to investigate how the position of the Sun changes the length of a shadow during a sunny day.

Resources

❖ Metre stick or other suitable stick, bucket of sand, chalk, clock/watch.

Safety! Protect the top of the stick with a cork or Plasticine ball.

Introduction: *Whole class session*

Ask children how shadows are formed and how they might change during the course of a day. Explain that they are going to investigate how the length of shadow created by the Sun on a metre stick changes during a day. Discuss ways of recording. What ideas do children have? If no one offers using a table, teach them how a table can help them plan the order of the investigation, the number of measurements that need to be made as well as giving a record of all findings. Draw a format possibly like this:

Time of day	Length of shadow (cm)
9.30 am	
12.00	
1.30	
3.30	

Group or individual activities

Children in small groups go into the playground to set up their shadow sticks. They record the time when each measurement was taken and length of the shadow in cm, i.e. quantitatively. They mark the shadow and time on the tarmac with chalk. This is repeated at intervals throughout the day.

Plenary session

Use the table of results to collect measurements from children. Help children compare measurements from different groups, helping them to see patterns. Explain that this information can be presented as a bar chart to tell the story of what happened during the day. Draw a bar chart and ask questions such as:

❖ How many times did you measure the shadow?
❖ When was it shortest?
❖ When was it longest?
❖ How long do you think it would be at 6.00pm?
❖ Why was it shortest at about midday?
❖ When are shadows shortest and longest?
❖ Would the shadow always be the same length at noon? Why?

Children are asked for homework to research from books with parents/carers, answers that could not be given, and to report back later in the week.

Points for assessment

❖ Do the children understand how to use a table?
❖ Can they measure length accurately using a metre ruler?
❖ Do they know that shadows are shortest at midday and longest early and late in the day?
❖ Do they connect these changes with the position of the Sun in the sky?

Teacher's own notes:

Lesson focus: *Earth and beyond*

KS2 NC Ref: *Sc1 2b, c, f, h–j; Sc4 4b*   **Year group:** *Y5/6*

Scheme of work unit: *5E – Earth, Sun and Moon*

Intended learning: for children to know that the Sun is a source of light for the Earth and if light from the Sun is blocked it goes darker; to know that is dangerous to look directly at the Sun.

Resources
❖ Paper, scissors, paint.
❖ Pictures of the Sun.
❖ Plotting compass.

Introduction: *Whole class session*

Show the children pictures of the Sun. Elicit their ideas about what it is and how it moves. Encourage them to raise questions about things they would like to know about the Sun, e.g. How big is it? How hot is it? Move the discussion on to how the Sun appears to move during a day. Seek children's ideas about how they could explore this idea. Some may suggest observing and recording where the Sun is in the sky at different times of the day. If possible select key landmarks that are mostly south facing and visible from the classroom window or nearby. Sketch some of these on the board, e.g. a prominent tree, nearby house/factory/church/hill. Mark the east, south and west positions using a compass if necessary. Observe where the Sun appears to be. Do not look directly at the Sun as this can damage the eyes. Invite a child to add the Sun to the drawing where it appears to be and add the date and time by it. Explain that the position will be recorded at different times of the day and in different seasons. To record this the class needs to make a large wall display. This will also enable the position of the Sun to be tracked at different seasons of the year.

Group or individual activities

Groups are allocated different aspects of the local landscape to draw and paint. Aspects are checked with a compass and added to the display after checking with the teacher. Groups take it in turns to monitor the Sun's position and add one to the appropriate part of the display.

This can be repeated in contrasting seasons, e.g. autumn, winter, spring and summer. Children use books, CD ROMs, etc, to research why the Sun appears to move and why it has a different position in the sky for the same time of day in contrasting seasons.

Plenary session

Use the display made from the first day's observations. Help children consider the evidence by asking:

❖ How does the Sun appear to move across the sky?
❖ When is the Sun at its highest point?
❖ When is the Sun at its lowest point?
❖ What do we call these times of the day?
❖ Where do you think the Sun would be at the same times if we repeated this at another time of the year (summer/winter)?
❖ How could you check your predictions?

For further research, ask the children to find out for homework if it is the Sun or Earth which moves.

Points for assessment

❖ What do the children know about the Sun?
❖ Do the children know that the Sun rises in the east at dawn?
❖ Can they plot its apparent movement across the sky?
❖ Do they know it is noon when the Sun is in the south at its highest point in the sky?
❖ Do they know that in the afternoon the Sun appears to sink lower into the sky until it sets at sunset?
❖ Can they research information to plot the apparent movement of the Sun in a contrasting season?

Teacher's own notes:

Index